GIVING AND RECEIVING PERFORMANCE FEEDBACK

Peter R. Garber

South Country Library
22 Station Road
Bellport, NY 11713

DEC 27 2005

HRD Press, Inc. • Amherst • Mas:

D1367928

Copyright © 2004, Peter R. Garber

All rights reserved. No part of this book may be reproduced in any form without written permission from the publisher. International rights and foreign translations are available only through negotiations of a licensing agreement with the publisher.

Published by: HRD Press, Inc.
                 22 Amherst Road
                 Amherst, MA 01002
                 800-822-2801 (U.S. and Canada)
                 413-253-3488
                 413-253-3490 (fax)
                 http://www.hrdpress.com

ISBN 0-87425-773-5

Printed in Canada

Production services by Jean Miller
Editorial services by Sally Farnham
Cover design by Donna Thibault-Wong

Contents

CONTENTS

Introduction
The Good News and the Bad News

Even in today's age of communication, there are still many messages we do not want to receive. For example, truthfully, most people would prefer not to receive feedback on how they are performing their job. It is not the positive aspects of performance evaluation that we dread, but rather the negative. Receiving this kind of feedback threatens our self-image, ego, and perhaps even our motivation. In virtually any organization, it would not be difficult to find any number of employees who feel they have been unfairly evaluated concerning their job performance. One might ask the following questions: If all this negative feedback is causing so many problems, then why continue to provide it? What is it that we think we are accomplishing by providing this type of feedback? On the other hand, what happens if people never hear the negative side of their performance? They might indeed be far less threatened by not hearing negative feedback, but will they really be receiving all the information they need to know about their performance?

In ancient Persia, killing the bearer of bad news was standard practice. We refer to the present-day version of this ancient ritual as "shooting the messenger"; we transfer our negative feelings about the information we receive to the person who was unfortunate enough to be the one who delivered the bad news. We mistakenly believe that "shooting the messenger" will make the problem go away. After withstanding the brunt of delivering bad news once or twice, it doesn't take long for people to learn *not* to be the bearers of bad tidings if they can possibly avoid it. All this can lead to a non-productive performance feedback system containing nothing but "happy talk" that describes only a relatively narrow spectrum of a person's performance. This will obviously do little to help the individual receiving the feedback improve his or her performance and grow personally and professionally.

Chapter 1

The Annual Performance Review

Most people have experienced (or shall we say, survived) the annual performance review process in one form or another during their careers. We tend to think of performance feedback as being in the form of an annual evaluation in which your performance is measured against pre-established criteria. A standard form or format is usually followed with checklist-type criteria measuring the individual's performance against the organization standards. Although this tried-and-true method has served to provide performance feedback to employees for many years—even decades—there are also many inherent problems with this approach. Possibly its greatest limitation is that this type of feedback is typically received only once a year.

Now this is not to say or even suggest that annual performance-review systems are not useful or meaningful; on the contrary, they serve as a cornerstone to any performance-feedback system an organization might have. There are many other systems that often emanate from these evaluations. For example, the entire salaried merit distribution plan is often based on the annual performance review that people receive from their supervisor. In addition, many career-altering decisions such as promotions, transfers, job placements, out-placements, selections, and rejections are typically based on a person's annual performance review.

So then why consider doing anything different than the traditional annual performance appraisal? One possible reason is that the traditional approach addresses only a small slice of an individual's overall job performance. Another reason: The aspects that are included in these reviews may or may not have any real meaning or value to the individual being evaluated. *Giving and Receiving Performance Feedback* explores the limitations of traditional evaluation systems and how they might be addressed and improved. In addition, alternative approaches are introduced in later chapters, including a new concept, *self-directed feedback.*

Setting Performance Goals

Before beginning any discussion on performance feedback, it is important to stress that there are no absolutes concerning this subject—there are no right or wrong approaches to providing feedback. What is most important is what fits the needs, expectations, and goals of the organization and its employees. A good way to begin is to ask yourself the question, "What are your goals and objectives concerning performance feedback in your organization?"

Giving performance feedback just for the sake of it or just going through the motions of performance evaluation will obviously not be beneficial to the organization. This, however, is contrary to popular belief in many organizations. It is often believed that as long as there is a performance feedback system of some kind in place, then people will receive the information they need to perform their jobs to their greatest potential. Unfortunately, this reasoning is flawed.

As a starting point, complete the following brief questionnaire concerning performance feedback in your organization. As you continue through this book, use your answers as a baseline for where you find yourself and the organization concerning the giving and receiving of performance feedback.

Performance Feedback Questionnaire

1. Are there any established goals and objectives for performance feedback in your organization? If so, list them below.

_____

_____

_____

_____

_____

2. Are these goals supportive of the performance feedback that people receive in your organization? In other words, do they help people improve their performance? Why or why not?

_____

_____

_____

_____

_____

3. Are these goals exclusive? That is, do they exclude certain groups of employees from benefiting from reaching these goals and rewards? How?

_____

_____

_____

_____

_____

Performance Feedback Questionnaire (continued)

4. Is performance feedback tied to or part of other personnel-related processes in the organization? Which ones?

    _____

    _____

    _____

    _____

    _____

5. What other methods or ways do people receive feedback about their performance on the job?

    _____

    _____

    _____

    _____

    _____

6. Referring to your answer to Question 5, which of these sources of performance feedback have the greatest influence on people? Why?

    _____

    _____

    _____

    _____

    _____

Performance Feedback Questionnaire (continued)

Performance Feedback Goals

Based on your responses to these questions, think about what goals you would hope to achieve from receiving performance feedback in your organization:

Organizational Goals	Personal Goals
_____	_____
_____	_____
_____	_____
_____	_____
_____	_____
_____	_____
_____	_____
_____	_____
_____	_____
_____	_____
_____	_____
_____	_____
_____	_____
_____	_____

Performance Feedback Questionnaire (continued)

Skill-Building Questions

Are these goals compatible? How?

_____

_____

_____

_____

_____

_____

_____

_____

Are these goals incompatible? How?

_____

_____

_____

_____

_____

_____

_____

_____

Chapter 2

Making Performance Feedback Meaningful

Making performance feedback meaningful to both the individual and the organization should be the ultimate objective in any efforts to improve in this area. If it is not meaningful to either the individual or the organization, performance feedback will fall into the same trap of many other communications programs: It will become a routine exercise that everyone goes through in which little or no benefit is gained. The typical performance appraisal becomes just another dreaded experience that must be repeated at least once a year. It is viewed with the same enthusiasm as going to the dentist and might even be perceived as being more painful—sort of like getting your teeth drilled without Novocain!

The challenge for any organization is changing performance feedback from something that might be currently looked at with the same emotion as getting a root canal to something that is perceived as a personal opportunity for growth and development that will add value to the entire organization. Let's continue this discussion with a look at some of the common problems that many organizations experience in their performance feedback systems.

10 Common Pitfalls of Performance Feedback Systems

1. **Performance feedback in the organization is given only during annual performance evaluations.** Inherent in these programs is the fact that feedback is provided only once a year. The very definition of an annual performance evaluation is descriptive of the problem: Once

a year is usually just not often enough to give people adequate feedback about their performance. People need to hear how they are doing, both positive and negative, on a regular basis. If the only time a person hears anything about their job performance is once a year, they are being "left in the dark" about how they are doing on a daily basis. They are likely participating in a performance-feedback system with the philosophy: "If you don't hear anything about how you are performing your job, you are doing just fine. I'll let you know when you screw up!" Typically in an environment that practices this philosophy, if a person does make a mistake, he or she doesn't receive any feedback about it until their annual performance evaluation. That is unless it is a big mistake, then watch out—KA-BOOM! Obviously, performance feedback needs to be given on an ongoing basis throughout the year. This is the only way that a person can realistically be expected to grow and develop in their job.

2. **Performance appraisals are based on a single evaluator's feedback.** A common practice is for the reference source of the performance feedback to be from only one perspective—that of the person's supervisor. The pitfall to this typical approach is that there can be many factors that influence the supervisor's perception of the individual that are unrelated to his or her actual job performance. These can include any biases, conflicts, philosophical differences, jealousies, rivalries, etc., that might exist on any level between the supervisor and the individual being appraised. Even when these negative types of factors do not exist, there can still be the problem of supervisors not having the time to be able to adequately understand how the person is performing his or her job. Supervisors might have any number of subordinates for whom they have the responsibility of evaluating. The very scope of their responsibilities might preclude them from giving formal feedback to their subordinates any more frequently than once a year. Even this often becomes a challenge for many supervisors to accomplish.

3. **Feedback is presented only by the supervisor.** Single-source performance feedback is likewise typically *presented* by a single person—the individual's supervisor. Although this might be a perfectly acceptable arrangement for everyone in many cases, there might be drawbacks in other situations. If problems such as those mentioned previously exist, they become magnified when presented by the supervisor. For example, if a person feels that the supervisor doesn't like him or her, everything that is presented in the performance evaluation will be filtered through this perception. It doesn't really matter if the person's perceptions about their supervisor's feelings are right or wrong: The message the person hears is still the same. Even sincere attempts by the supervisor to give accurate feedback to the individual can be tainted by these perceptions: "The boss is just saying that about me because she doesn't like me" or "He just said I did a good job on that project because he knows that everyone has been saying that, and he didn't want to look like he doesn't know what's going on." Even in the most optimal of situations where the supervisor and the subordinate have a good working relationship, performance is seen only from one perspective. There are obviously many other dimensions of the individual's job performance that cannot be seen from only the supervisor's vantage point.

4. **Performance evaluations are more of an argument built to support the overall performance rating that is being given.** Defending or justifying the rating given to the individual becomes the main objective rather than providing meaningful feedback. Sometimes it might seem that a performance evaluation is nothing more than a case built against the individual to justify the rating that has been pronounced upon him or her. The supervisor spends more time on explaining his or her rationale for rating the person the way he or she did than on anything else during the review. Just as most guilty verdicts are read to defendants who still maintain their innocence, it is unlikely that anyone can ever be convinced that their lower performance ratings are justified

by the evidence presented to them by their supervisor. A supervisor is not the prosecuting attorney, and the person being evaluated is not on the witness stand. Do not turn the performance review into a courtroom drama. Doing so makes the performance review more negatively based than developmental.

5. **Performance feedback is negatively based.** Performance feedback is often full of "gotchas"—"I 'gotcha' doing this wrong" or "I 'gotcha' making this mistake" is all the person hears. A "gotcha" is when a supervisor finds something that someone did wrong and saves it to be presented to him or her during their annual performance evaluation. "Gotchas" have a much more dramatic effect on the individual when they are stored into an "arsenal" to maximize the force of their impact to create one huge KA-BOOM!

6. **Performance feedback addresses only the formal aspects of job performance.** Annual performance feedback reviews typically address how an individual performed against some predetermined goals or objectives. There are other aspects of one's performance that usually do not get mentioned in this type of structured and formal review. These might appear to be trivial things that do not seem to merit mentioning in the context of presenting a person's overall performance rating. Annual performance evaluations usually focus on the results of an individual's efforts during the past year. They do not usually address the behaviors involved in achieving these desired results. Often these are the things that people make the greatest personal sacrifices to achieve and of which they are proudest. These include many extra efforts that too often go unrecognized, such as coming in early to work and staying late, covering for co-workers during their absences, and working through sicknesses and personal problems, just to name a few.

7. **Performance feedback is tied to raises/Performance feedback is not tied to raises.** This is obviously a double-edged sword; there are as many inherent problems with systems that tie performance evaluations to merit raises as there are in systems that do not. Tying these two systems together has the potential of rewarding and motivating people by giving them more money for achieving greater levels of performance.

   Unfortunately, merit raise systems don't always meet this goal:

   - People don't always perceive that there is a direct link between compensation and their performance.

   - The goals and criteria for achieving financial rewards might not be defined well enough to be motivational.

   - The "payoff" for achieving these higher performance levels might not be seen as being worth the price of working harder to achieve.

   - People might feel that the "deck" is stacked against them concerning their performance rating; for any number of reasons, they might believe that regardless of what effort they make, they will still be evaluated the same way. Unfortunately, in many cases, this might be true.

   If raises are not tied to performance reviews, there can be a complete disconnect between rewards and performance. There are systems where everyone is compensated according to some set schedule regardless of their performance. The "across-the-board" raise approach might take much of the politics and game playing out of the performance compensation system, but also might not be very motivational.

8. **Performance feedback is not specific enough about the person's performance.** People want and need to have specific details about how they are perceived and evaluated. A performance appraisal needs to include very specific information about the individual being evaluated.

"Are you sure you are talking about me?" should not be a question asked by a person being evaluated! A supervisor should be prepared to give specific examples—both good and bad as appropriate—relating to the person's performance. Simply saying to someone "You are not doing a good job" does nothing to help the person improve their performance in the future. The very first thing that the person will say is, "Give me a specific example of my not doing a good job." If you can't provide such examples, you will have accomplished nothing constructive by bringing up negative feedback during the evaluation.

Similarly, mentioning specific examples concerning desired job performance will almost guarantee that they will be repeated in the future.

9. **Formal performance reviews are full of surprises.** People should not be surprised by any information presented in their formal performance evaluations. Surprises are fun if they are a gift or a party in your honor, but not if they occur during your performance review or evaluation. If you as a supervisor have done a good job of communicating performance feedback to your subordinates throughout the year, there really should not be any entirely new information presented during the annual performance review. You should not pull out a list of "gotchas" that you have collected all year on the person. Summary and review rather than surprise should be your guide in conducting an annual performance review.

10. **The design of many performance appraisal systems results in making 80 percent of those affected by them mad!** Most typical performance appraisal systems have guidelines or restrictions on the percentage of people that can be slotted into various rating categories. The focus of the approach is to prevent too many people from being given the top performance rating. It is believed that if everyone is rated in the top performance category, it will lose its value and significance. Because many performance appraisal systems set limits on the number

of people that can be evaluated in the highest category, there can be many hard feelings as a result. Typically, no more than 20 to 25 percent of those being evaluated are permitted to receive the highest rating. (This results in a bell-shaped performance rating distribution curve phenomenon, which will be discussed in more detail later in this book.) The result is that the remaining majority of the people in the evaluation system feel excluded. Most people take a great deal of pride in the work they perform and are upset when they don't receive recognition for their efforts in the form of these higher ratings. Perhaps it is because work becomes such a big part of a person's life that anything less than the highest rating is perceived as a failure to them.

Chapter 3

Feedback Models

Meaningful performance feedback is best achieved by understanding the interaction between the feedback *giver* and the feedback *receiver*. (Please note: The participants in the presentation of performance feedback were intentionally not designated as the supervisor giving feedback to the subordinate. Although this is a common model for providing feedback, it is by no means the only possible one. Other alternatives to providing feedback will be covered throughout this book.)

Regardless of who presents the feedback to the receiver, there are perceptual barriers that these communications must pass through. These barriers act as filters that can affect the actual message that is heard. Each person has their own "perceptual filters" that "color" the feedback they receive. What determines a person's perceptual filters for receiving feedback? The answer is they are as varied and individualized as are people. To illustrate, let's say that a person perceives (correctly or incorrectly) that their supervisor doesn't like him or her. This perception becomes a filtering device that influences the meaning of everything that his or her supervisor says in the form of performance feedback or in any other interaction they have.

For example, let's say that a supervisor needs to give someone feedback on a project that did not meet all the requirements that were necessary for the job to be completed correctly. As in the earlier example, this person has the perception that the supervisor doesn't like him and is always trying to make things more difficult for him. The person will rationalize the supervisor's feedback through his perceptual filter by saying, "The reason my supervisor said that the project I just completed didn't meet all the requirements is because he doesn't like me."

In Figure 1, a number of variables of performance feedback are plugged into a feedback model. The variable for both the giver and the receiver of feedback will be determined by the perceptions of the participants. Figure 1 lists only a few of the limitless possible variables that these perceptions can create.

Figure 1. Feedback Model

GIVER	PERCEPTIONS	RECEIVER
Biases		Receptivity
Security		Growth
Experience		Commitment
Communications		Goals
Sensitivity		Self-Esteem
Expectations		Motivators
Values		Values

Now in Figure 2, begin developing your own feedback model with yourself as a giver or receiver of feedback. Think back to the most recent performance feedback session in which you participated. Fill in the variables for each side of the perceptual filter (i.e., your perceptions and what you believe were the other participant's perceptions).

Figure 2. Your Feedback Model

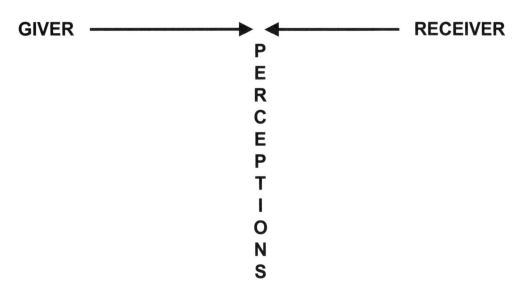

The main point here is that performance feedback must break through these perception barriers. If not, we will always be held prisoner by them. If we can never truly understand what is being said, heard, meant, or felt in the feedback we receive, we will not be able to use this potentially valuable information to grow both personally and professionally.

The Said/Heard—Meant/Felt Feedback Matrix

The Said/Heard—Meant/Felt Matrix in Figure 3 should help give more clarity to the concepts introduced in Figures 1 and 2. If you had difficulty completing Figure 2, you might want to go back to it after reviewing this matrix.

Figure 3. Said/Heard—Meant/Felt Feedback Matrix

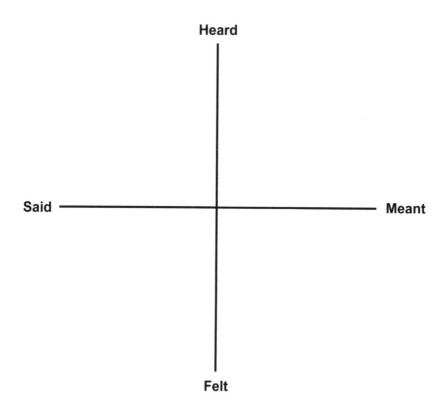

The Said/Heard—Meant/Felt Matrix can be used in many ways and directions. For example, it can be applied vertically, horizontally, counter clockwise, and clockwise. It can also begin at any point on the matrix. It can be used by either the giver or the receiver of performance feedback or both. However, its most effective use would be realized when all the participants in the performance feedback process use it.

To illustrate how it works, let's start by using the matrix in a clockwise direction beginning at the 9:00 o'clock position. From this point we begin with what is "Said." (Because we have chosen to travel clockwise in the matrix, we will label the four quadrants A, B, C, and D as shown in Figure 4.)

Figure 4. Said/Heard—Meant/Felt Quadrants

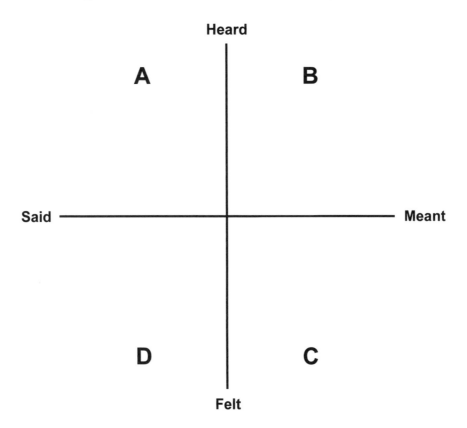

Now, let's look at how the matrix could be used to gain a better understanding of what might be discussed during a typical performance review. We will begin in Figure 5 with what is "Said."

Figure 5. Quadrant A

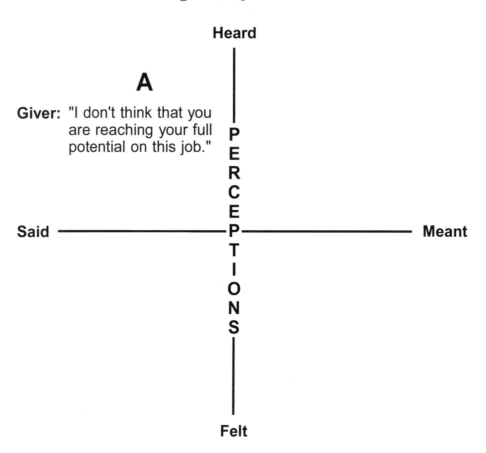

In Quadrant A, the feedback giver has said, "I don't think that you are reaching your full potential on this job." This statement must now pass through the perceptions barrier that is seen as the vertical axis of the matrix. What is heard by the receiver is illustrated in Quadrant B in Figure 6.

Figure 6. Quadrant B

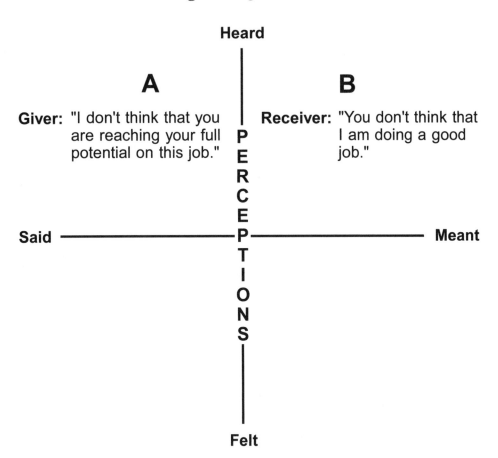

After passing through the receiver's perceptual barrier, you can see in Quadrant B that what was heard was "You don't think that I am doing a good job." This may or may not have been what the feedback giver "meant." In Figure 7, Quadrant C, the giver clarifies for the receiver the intended meaning of his Quadrant A statement.

Figure 7. Quadrant C

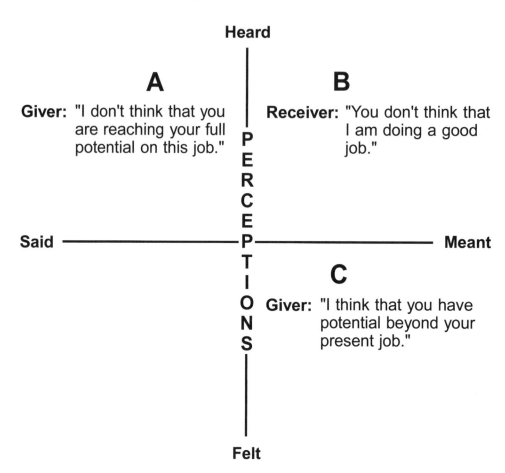

In Quadrant C, the feedback giver's meaning was very different than the receiver perceived. The receiver's feeling concerning this feedback is shown in Quadrant D in Figure 8.

Figure 8. Quadrant D

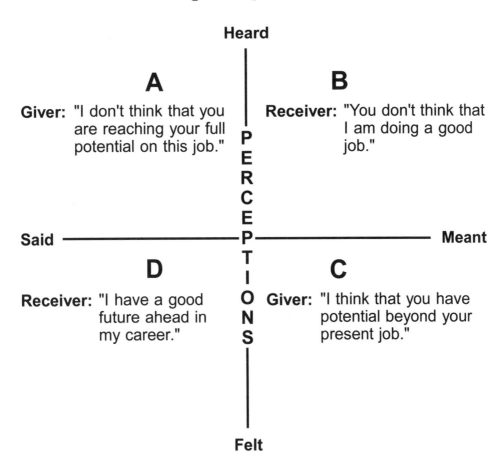

Heard

A

Giver: "I don't think that you are reaching your full potential on this job."

B

Receiver: "You don't think that I am doing a good job."

Said ——————— **PERCEPTIONS** ——————— **Meant**

D

Receiver: "I have a good future ahead in my career."

C

Giver: "I think that you have potential beyond your present job."

Felt

Utilizing the Matrix

There is a dramatic contrast between what the receiver perceived the performance feedback message to be in Quadrant B versus Quadrant D. The problem in many performance review sessions is that the communications end at Quadrant B. These misinterpretations can be very counterproductive and will not support the goals and objectives of providing feedback. It might be better to give no feedback until these misunderstandings are reconciled.

Use the Said/Heard—Meant/Felt Feedback Matrix during your next performance review session. Fill in or discuss each of the quadrants of the matrix as you go through the session. The dialog might go something like this: "You have heard my feedback on your performance. Now tell me what you just think you heard." After listening to the receiver's Quadrant B response, the giver clarifies what he said: "Well now I understand how you perceived that, but what I really meant was this…. How do you feel about this now?" The giver listens to the receiver's Quadrant D response.

The matrix can also be used by the receiver to get clarification on points that were not made clear during the performance review. As mentioned earlier, the matrix can be utilized in any direction. For example, say that the receiver has heard and interpreted something said in a performance review at a Quadrant B level. The person could go back to the giver and say, "Did I hear you correctly when you said…." This would prompt the giver to restate his or her Quadrant A and C positions leading to Quadrant D clarification and understanding for the receiver.

We need to break through our perceptual barriers to really begin to understand what is being said, heard, meant, and felt when presenting performance feedback. There can be a tremendous difference between what is said (intended) and what is felt (interpreted). It is in this void that the greatest opportunities to improve your current performance feedback and appraisal practices exist. If you were to do nothing more than have people in your organization leave their annual performance review sessions with a Quadrant D level of understanding rather than Quadrant B, you will have made significant progress in improving the quality of feedback that people are receiving. However, you don't have to stop here. Other challenges for you to undertake in order to improve the feedback people receive will be reviewed in the chapters that follow.

Chapter 4

Feedback
Perspectives

In Chapter 3, we looked at how people's different perceptions influence their understanding of the performance feedback they receive. Now let's look at how people's perspectives affect this understanding as well. In this discussion, there can be some definite blurring of the lines between perception and perspective. For purposes of clarity, let's make some basic distinctions. Perceptions involve how we interpret the messages we receive, and perspective is how we see these messages.

Does everyone in a typical organization—except the fortunate 20 percent of the entire employee population that receive the highest performance ratings—perceive performance feedback as one big KA-BOOM? If so, there is little chance that it is being very effective from either a development or motivational standpoint. Does this type of rating system cause resentment and even sabotage of the "chosen few"? Do the other 80 percent not included in this coveted category have a "Mom always liked you best" complex? Again, what are the consequences of a performance appraisal system inherently designed to make 80 percent of its participants mad about how they were evaluated? What perspective does this cause everyone to have concerning performance feedback in the organization?

The Leverage Perspective

Leverage is what drives the business world. Without it, you have no influence. Leverage is what you have control over to make others do what you want them to do. Leverage is power. Having the power to evaluate someone else's job performance can be awesome; it can give you tremendous leverage over other people. As mentioned, in most organizations, how an individual's job performance is evaluated affects any number of the very important variables in their career development (or lack thereof). Understandably, subordinates feel this tremendous leverage exerted by their bosses. This can have a definite perspective-changing influence on how the person views any performance feedback he or she might receive from their supervisor.

The question here becomes, "Does performance feedback always have to be leveraged with consequences, either positive or negative?" Can there be such a thing as non-consequential feedback? We will explore, in greater detail, variations of this type of feedback in the discussions of 360-degree feedback and self-directed feedback in Chapters 6 and 7, respectively. Immediately apparent in these forms of performance feedback is that the employee's supervisor does not present the feedback. This disconnects much of the leverage associated with supervisor-generated performance feedback people typically receive. But is feedback as effective if it is not received by the supervisor? Without leverage will it still have meaning? Will it still motivate people to change their job performance behavior?

Should the supervisor have access to their employee's peer-provided feedback in order to develop a more accurate employee evaluation? Should these alternative sources of performance feedback be included in the formal rating process? There are no absolute right or wrong answers to these questions. They are presented simply to make you more aware and sensitive to the issues associated with providing performance feedback in your organization. The concept of increasing or decreasing the leverage associated with performance feedback needs to be decided by each organization, taking into full consideration the culture, norms, practices, expectations, and objectives that exist. Keep in mind that all these factors will have a significant influence on the perspective of how everyone sees performance feedback in your organization.

Matters of Degree

The answer to almost all the questions asked about how to give performance feedback is "It depends." It depends on the particular organization and its goals for performance feedback. More than anything else, it is probably a matter of degree in the performance feedback systems of most organizations. Virtually everything discussed in this book most likely exists to some degree in any organization; it is just a matter of how formal or developed these concepts might be.

This can work both ways. Even the most effective performance feedback systems can have some negative elements. They might not "kill the messenger," but they might wound him a little! You might not hear KA-BOOMS, but perhaps "pops" instead! Regardless of the degree, these events can have a dramatic effect on the perspective that people have on performance feedback.

The Politics of Performance Feedback

The term *politics* conjures up many thoughts and memories. We think of presidential campaigns and political conventions with all their pageantry, circus atmosphere, and promises for the future. We also see a great deal of strategy and positioning of people to where they think they can optimize their influence. Everyone is looking to gain something. Unfortunately, not everybody will get what they want despite the campaign promises that were made to them along the way. Who makes these political decisions concerning who is in and who is out in the campaign and after the election? How does this political process work?

Whether you're talking about who gets the vice-presidential nod at the party's national convention or who receives the highest performance ratings at work, these "political" processes can be very similar. Those who are in positions of influence will make these decisions based on any number of factors. Some of these factors might be directly related to the individual's ability and performance. Other considerations might be for reasons completely unrelated to job performance: Factors such as who a supervisor likes best, who a person works for, and even who a person might be related to can become important non-performance–related factors in evaluations.

The amount of faith people have in the objectivity and fairness of the performance review system will be a function of the degree to which they perceive politics playing a role in ratings decisions. Unfortunately, few organizations are conscious of this aspect of their performance evaluation systems.

Skill-Building Question

How do you think employees perceive politics as playing a role in how their job performance is evaluated?

_____

_____

_____

_____

_____

_____

_____

_____

_____

_____

_____

Halo and Horns Revisited

The halo-and-horns effects have been influential in how employees are perceived by their supervisors for many years. As the name implies, the halo effect casts a favorable light on the individual, while the horns effect casts a negative one. A person perceived with a halo can do little wrong in the eyes of his or her supervisor. Any problems that might exist in this person's performance are caused by the other people and events that surround him or her. This "glow" can transcend any deficiencies the person might have in performing his or her job. The halo effect can perpetuate high ratings for employees regardless of their present performance. Sometimes it can be very difficult for an employee to lose their "angel wings" once they are bestowed upon them.

Similarly, the horns effect can be equally if not more difficult to shed. Once an employee gets on the "wrong side" of his or her boss, this perception of the person can be virtually impossible to change. Everything the person does becomes tainted by this negative image. This perception can be spread to others throughout the organization, becoming like a "black cloud" that follows him or her around.

How real or imagined those biased perceptions are is usually anybody's guess. There is probably a large degree of truth in both perceptual extremes of people. The problem is the inflexibility that typically accompanies these perceptual viewpoints. This "labeling" process causes people to be placed in categories (both good and bad) from which they cannot escape no matter how they perform in the future. This problem is typically created and maintained by a single person who is usually in a position of influence in the organization. As long as this person is in power, the halo-or-horns effects will be perpetuated. Contradictory evidence about the individual will be immediately dismissed as merely "flukes" and not really indicative of the person's behavior or performance.

Is there really any basis to justify these opinions and categorization of people? There very well may be, but the real fallacy in this thinking is that it does not take into account the fact that people can change. This is even more true if you are looking at an individual over a long period of time. A halo or horns placed upon someone early on could impact their entire career.

Organizations often keep a "book" of sorts on people in the organization. This book is typically more unofficial than official and is not necessarily in written form. It is more a reflection of the perceptions that the organization has about its people. This book is a collection of opinions on the individual that can be passed down from one generation of management to the next. The way people are perceived can be as much a function of the political powers in office in the organization than any other factors.

Skill-Building Questions

Is there a "book" on employees in your workplace? How can this book be "shut" or thrown away?

_____

_____

_____

_____

_____

How can people be given a fresh start in their careers, even if they have been performing their jobs for a long time?

_____

_____

_____

_____

_____

The Aesop Fable

There is an Aesop Fable that goes like this: A stranger was walking along a country road when he saw a farmer working in his field. The stranger asked the farmer if there was a town nearby in which he could settle. When told that there was a village a few miles down the road he asked, "What kind of people will I find there?" The farmer wisely replied, "What kind of people did you find where you came from? You will find the same kind of people here."

This story illustrates the important point that it is the individual who ultimately determines how others feel about him or her. You can blame politics or favoritism for not getting the rating you think you deserve, but if you do, you have let them "beat you." You should never give up trying to do the best job you possibly can. Ultimately, people get what they work for and deserve in this world. To do otherwise would be to admit defeat without a fight!

Negative Feedback

Receiving negative feedback about one's job performance is definitely a perspective-changing experience. It is intended to be. Presented properly, negative feedback can serve to help the person correct performance problems that could ultimately impact their future job security. When there are issues that need to be addressed, negative feedback needs to be part of the overall communications that people receive about themselves. Not addressing these problems would be an injustice to the individual by allowing him/her to continue to perform below standards with no indication that their work is unacceptable. This is really just another way of saving "gotchas."

These are the scenes when an unsuspecting "victim" is called into their boss's office one morning only to be told that after 27 years of loyal service to the company, they are being let go due to their performance. KA-BOOM! As the shocked employee's entire career flashes before his eyes, he is being handed a severance check and escorted to the front door into an awaiting taxi. He hears something about not being considered a top performer over the years and that as part of the company's recent down-sizing program, only the very best performers are being retained.

"Funny," he thinks to himself, "nobody ever mentioned that they weren't pleased with my work for the past 27 years," as the taxi speeds away.

Does this sound more like a scene out of a Woody Allen film than what goes on daily in our work world? As much as we would like to believe that this is something seen only in the movies, we all know better than that. This scene is played out over and over again in real life work situations. People receive little or no feedback about their deficiencies on the job until it is too late for them to do anything about it.

Why does this happen? The most obvious answer is that it is simply easier. Supervisors generally don't enjoy giving people negative feedback about their job performance any more than people like to receive it. Instead, supervisors tolerate poor performance rather than address and try to correct it. They also don't always suffer this sub-standard work in silence. They might complain to everyone except the poor performer about the quality of his or her work. When judgment day comes and the "ax" finally falls, no one is surprised except the person being terminated. KA-BOOM again. Is this really fair to the person in this case?

Giving and Receiving Feedback

When appropriate and presented correctly, negative feedback can be some of the most potentially valuable information about yourself that you might ever receive. Often, it is the feedback that is the most difficult to hear that allows us the most growth opportunity. With negative feedback, you need to keep an open mind and be willing to accept what you hear. No one (not even your boss) does a perfect job, making them subject to at least some negative feedback about their performance. The following are ways in which a supervisor can use negative feedback in the most positive ways possible.

Negative Feedback Guidelines

1.   Be knowledgeable about the individual's performance. Know exactly what performance you are addressing. As with any feedback, be prepared to give examples of the individual's poor performance. As mentioned before, you will be asked to provide this type of specific information.

2.   Give the person a chance to defend him- or herself. Don't rush too quickly to judgment before you have heard their side of the story. Listen to their reasons and rationale for their behavior and performance. Be willing to accept the fact that there might be factors beyond the person's control for these problems. Plan for ways to correct or address these factors to help the person improve his or her performance.

3.   Don't give the person a "mixed message." A mixed message is one where you hear two seemingly contradictory things at the same time. If you have a negative message to deliver to someone, then just do it! Don't try to sugarcoat it by wrapping it up in complimentary feedback and sandwiching it in between. This doesn't really "soften" the blow or make negative feedback any easier to accept. It will only serve to confuse the person more. Make it clear what performance needs to be improved and why. Don't have the person leave not knowing if he or she was told that they were doing a good job or a bad one.

   An example of a mixed negative feedback message might sound something like this:

> "I want to talk to you about your work on the new project. You have been doing a good job keeping everything on schedule so far. However, the accuracy of the numbers you have been providing seems to be way off. Accuracy is critical to the success of the entire project. Mistakes made now can cause us millions of dollars to correct later on. You need to ensure the

accuracy of your numbers from now on. By the way, I really enjoyed the update presentation you gave on the project the other day. I know everyone was very impressed with the job you are doing so far."

What message would this person leave this meeting hearing? Would it be that he or she is doing a good job or bad? One might argue that this person would feel that overall he or she was doing well, but had to concentrate on improving in one area—accuracy. However, the communications would be much clearer if these two types of feedback were given on separate occasions. They could be given on the same day, but not at the same time. This way, the importance of the accuracy of the data would not be diluted by the other information, and there would be a greater chance of the person understanding how his or her performance needs to improve. The positive feedback is equally important and should not be forfeited in order to deliver the negative to avoid a mixed message. KA-BOOM! If we fall into this trap, we are again back to the old style of performance feedback, "If you don't hear anything, you are doing just fine."

4. Be constructive. Negative feedback should be constructive in its intent. If the reason for delivering negative feedback is anything other than to constructively help the individual, then it should not be delivered. The person should be told the following concerning his or her unacceptable performance: Why the performance is not meeting requirements. What the person must do to improve this performance. How this performance will be measured and how improvements will be communicated to the person in the future. When the person's progress made toward the desired performance goals will be reviewed and how frequently.

5. Consequences need to be understood. People seem to fear the worst when they hear negative feedback about their performance. Negative feedback needs to include at least some discussion about its ultimate

consequences. If it is a "do or die" situation, then this needs to be told to the person. Similarly, if there are little or no consequences associated with this negative feedback, then this should be explained as well.

Finally, dramatizing the significance of negative feedback will not ultimately serve the supervisor very well. One can only cry "wolf" so many times before everyone becomes conditioned not to listen anymore. Of course, just as in the story, one day a real wolf might happen by and no one will respond to the cries for help.

Skill-Building Questions

Think about a past experience when you needed to give someone negative feedback.

How do you feel about giving this type of feedback?

_____

_____

_____

_____

_____

_____

_____

_____

_____

Skill-Building Questions (continued)

What problems did you have delivering this type of feedback?

_____

_____

_____

_____

_____

_____

_____

_____

How could you have done this more effectively using the information just presented?

_____

_____

_____

_____

_____

_____

_____

_____

Skill-Building Questions (continued)

If you had presented this information the way you just described, do you believe the results would have been different? Why?

_____

_____

_____

_____

_____

_____

_____

_____

Chapter 5

Feedback Consequences

Whenever you deliver feedback to people—particularly negative feedback—inevitably, there are going to be consequences. People can be very sensitive about any type of criticism they receive about themselves. You need to look at a person's performance from their perspective. Employees might focus on different things than their supervisor would. People remember the personal sacrifices they had to make to meet the responsibilities of their jobs. These sacrifices are often taken for granted by supervisors. From the employees' perspective, the payback for all their efforts is oftentimes nothing but criticism. KA-BOOM!

As a result, employees might begin to view their jobs negatively. They begin to feel that no one appreciates their extra efforts to try to do a good job and eventually stop putting forth any extra effort. Sometimes they learn to minimally perform their jobs, doing only what they must to keep out of trouble and stay employed. They rationalize their minimal efforts as being commensurate with the amount of reinforcement they receive from their employer. In many circumstances, there might be justification for this rationalization; people respond to the environment in which they exist. If their work environment contains nothing except negative feedback, how can they be expected to be motivated to do a better job?

Formal and Informal Recognition

As mentioned in the Pitfalls of Performance Feedback in Chapter 2, money may or may not play a major role in this lack of motivation. Money definitely plays a role in those circumstances where the level of pay is inappropriately low for the job being performed. As Hertzburg described in his theory of "hygiene" factors in the workplace, certain things such as money serve only as a "dissatisfier," not as a "satisfier." In other words, pay can easily become a negative factor, but is seldom a great motivator.

Naturally, everyone would like to make more money for the job they perform. However, in many cases, money is probably not the primary cause of job dissatisfaction. Most likely, it is the lack of recognition for the good work that people do that is the greatest source of dissatisfaction and complaints. This recognition that employees desire can come in many forms, formal and informal. Recognition can be formal such as reward programs that honor outstanding performance. These programs are usually very visible. They might involve ceremonies, dinners, publicity, plaques, etc. Typically, this type of formal recognition is presented by some higher-ranking official in the organization to the individuals receiving the honor.

All this is a form of performance feedback, telling those receiving this recognition that they have done a good job. But what about other people who have also worked hard, but might not be so fortunate to be selected for this recognition? How many others not recognized view this recognition with some degree of jealousy or even contempt?

What is the consequence of these feelings? Do you think people with these envious feelings will be more motivated to work harder in the future to be similarly recognized? Or might they fall into that syndrome that rationalizes poorer performance? The answer will be as different as each circumstance in which this situation might occur. What is most important is to be conscious of when and where this scenario might become a reality. It is important that we think about all the possible consequences to any type of performance feedback we give to people throughout the organization.

What role does informal recognition play in performance feedback? Informal recognition includes all those ways people might receive feedback that do not require executive approval in order for it to be provided. That is the real beauty of informal recognition: It is always available and doesn't require a great deal of money to provide. In most situations, employees will say that it is the informal recognition they receive from their supervisor and co-workers that is most meaningful to them. "I just want someone to recognize the extra efforts I take to do my job" is how many people feel about their role in the organization. Informal recognition can come in many different forms limited only by your imagination.

Informal recognition can be a simple thank-you, a cup of coffee, a note or letter, a phone call, acknowledgment at a meeting, a bulletin board posting, and many other things. Regardless of how informal recognition is presented, the most important thing is that it is sincere. People would rather receive an informal acknowledgment that their efforts at work are recognized and appreciated than a formal award that does not have the same sincerity. Informal recognition can be very powerful performance feedback.

Ideally, an organization should have an appropriate balance of formal and informal recognition programs and processes. However, it is not unusual to hear that an organization feels that they do a good job of providing formal recognition and are not as effective in their informal recognition. Informal feedback is typically more personalized and face-to-face. As when giving any type of performance feedback, it is sometimes difficult for supervisors to express how they feel about the accomplishments of those who report to them, even when they want to recognize the good job they are doing. Thus, many excellent opportunities are not taken advantage of to provide people with what they need most concerning performance feedback/recognition.

The Psychological Effects of Performance Feedback

How much performance feedback is enough? How much is too much? In many ways, prescribing medicine is a perfect analogy for providing performance feedback: The dosage, time, and total amount to be given are all important factors to consider. The medicine also needs to be appropriate for the person receiving it. Too much medicine given at the wrong time can have serious consequences even if effective under different circumstances. Like prescribing medicine, you need to consider what the right amount of feedback is for each individual you provide it to. You can determine this by asking, "How much feedback can the person take?"

What are some of the psychological effects of performance feedback? The most obvious effect is the potential "labeling process" that is a result of many performance feedback systems. Labeling occurs when certain generalities and summary descriptions are assigned to individuals as part of the appraisal process. Most performance appraisal systems have rating categories, typically three to five in number. Not only can this rating assignment system cause those not placed in the highest category to become upset, it also stereotypes people. These labels can become like a "scarlet letter." Once a person has been labeled in a certain performance category, it might become more of a "life sentence" for the rest of their career. Not only does everyone who is associated with this process begin to respond to these labels, but even worse, so might the individual. The negative effects of this type of labeling process are clear. Certain expectations are established for people based on these labels. These expectations can create both limitations as well as unrealistic expectations about people's abilities and potential.

If a person has been labeled as being in an "average" category, everyone—including the individual—will most likely come to expect nothing more than this level of performance. Because the performance appraisal process is typically tied to other developmental opportunities in the organization, an average or poor rating might become like a diagnosis of a terminal career disease. The Pygmalion or self-fulfilling prophecy effect soon begins to take over: Because you expect only marginal or average performance from an individual, that is all you will ever get.

On the other hand, as was the case in the movie classic *My Fair Lady,* the Pygmalion effect can work in positive ways as well. People whose background and experience in no way qualify them for certain positions are given exceptional career opportunities and, despite their lack of credentials for the position, do an outstanding job. Every time this phenomenon occurs, one must wonder how many other people are out there who could meet similar challenges if only given the chance.

But what about the "other side" of promoting someone beyond their present qualifications? We have all witnessed individuals who have been placed in positions they were not truly prepared to accept. In many cases, the individual might not be aware of their deficiencies that could be a barrier to their success in the position. Perhaps they have never been given honest and accurate performance feedback that could have helped them be more successful in future job opportunities. They struggle unsuccessfully until everyone becomes frustrated to the point when action has to be taken to replace them with a more qualified person. Often, the "system" is quick to label this individual as a failure or disappointment. The individual is reassigned to a position with less responsibility, never to be looked at as having any growth potential again. The questions that should be asked in these circumstances are: Did this individual have all the necessary tools and resources at his or her disposal to meet the requirements of the job? Did he or she receive the feedback needed to adequately prepare for this challenge?

Sometimes people get punished for the inadequacies of the performance feedback system in their organizations. We often look for someone to blame for the system's failures rather than looking for ways to address the system's inadequacies. Performance feedback is often a good example of this problem. The design and structure of many typical performance feedback systems play right into this syndrome. These systems constantly label and relabel individuals as "winners" or "losers" based on their ability to work within the existing systems. These labels are typically not accurate representations of people's true abilities and talents, but rather merely a reflection of how well they are able to deal with the system.

There are many contradictory and confusing messages that people receive as a result of trying to succeed in these systems. Traditional work values and beliefs can become obscured by the dynamics of the typical performance appraisal and feedback systems today.

Truth Is a Point of View

In life, truth is a point of view. Or perhaps more accurately said, truth is a function of perspective. What might appear to be the truth to one person might be seen very differently by another. Truth is a personalized experience, and this becomes particularly evident in how people's work is evaluated. Just like the proverbial two sides to every argument, there are many ways of looking at a person's performance.

We choose both consciously and unconsciously to view performance in many different ways. As mentioned previously, there are many factors that influence these perceptions. The most fundamental of these perceptions might be our focus on the positive or negative aspects of an individual's job performance. This orientation can have a profound effect on a person's performance.

There was a classic study conducted a number of years ago in which an elementary school teacher was told that a certain group of her students were highly gifted and expected to perform above the rest of the class. In reality, this group was no more gifted than the rest of their peers. The point of the study was to see how the teacher's perceptions and expectations might influence these students' achievements. At the conclusion of the study, it was found that these students performed significantly better than their classmates who were not identified as high performers. We can conclude from this kind of data that the performance we might expect from people is the performance we ultimately get. We might never know just how much influence a supervisor's attitudes and expectations have on their subordinates' actual job performance. But we can say with certainty that they do play a major role.

Perceptions that "the boss doesn't like me" can have both rippling and long-term negative effects on a person's job performance. This syndrome that is constantly being experienced in virtually every workplace in the world might be responsible for more communication problems between supervisors and subordinates than any other single factor.

This can become the most formidable of all perceptual barriers between the boss and the subordinate. It will have a tremendous filtering effect on every word or action between them. This can become another example of a self-fulfilling prophecy: The person doesn't feel like their supervisor likes him or her, so they react negatively. This behavior causes the supervisor to think less of the person, and the syndrome begins to perpetuate itself. Truthfully, the supervisor most likely has no animosity or ill feelings toward the individual personally. What the supervisor really dislikes are the individual's negative reactions to anything he or she does or says.

Almost Perfect

When you really think about it, most people are almost perfect at performing their jobs. If they didn't function effectively nearly all the time, they probably would no longer be employed. People do so many aspects of their jobs correctly that it becomes expected. This level of performance might be a function of the repetition that is experienced performing a job over a long period of time, not to mention the talent and training people bring to their jobs. Whatever the reason, there is a certain level of proficiency that is expected of any job. In the quality process, we call this the performance standard. Our quality training has taught us that the goal must be 100 percent conformity to requirements.

Zero Defects is both a goal and concept that says anything less than perfect performance should not be acceptable. If we are not meeting this standard, then action must be taken to find out why and correct the problem to prevent it from recurring. Zero Defects, or 100 percent conformity to requirements, may or may not be realistically achieved on any given job. What is most important are the expectations that are established for performance on the job. If all you expect is 80 percent or even 95 percent of the job to be performed correctly, then that is all most people will ever aspire to achieve. That would be meeting the performance standard of the job. As a supervisor, you need to look closely at the performance standards you establish for those who work for you. Don't think for one moment that you don't set this performance standard. Even though you might have your subordinates establish their own goals and accountabilities for their jobs, it is ultimately your actions that determine their relative importance.

There is an old saying about work, "What gets done is that which the boss pays attention to." Early theories of management behavior would have said that this concept was true because the boss made sure the job got done correctly. Today we understand the concepts of positive reinforcement and that paying attention to people's work strengthens those behaviors. The concepts of positive reinforcement teach that to improve performance it is much more effective to reinforce the positive aspects of one's behaviors than it is to punish the negative. Positive reinforcement strengthens a person's behaviors, making it much more likely that they'll be repeated in the future. Punishment decreases performance, making it less likely that positive behaviors will be repeated in the future. Although some punishment might be necessary, it should be understood why it is being used and its possible effects on performance. Keeping in mind the fact that punishment decreases the likelihood of the behavior being repeated, you need to make sure that this is truly the desired result that you are trying to achieve.

Sometimes we unintentionally mix up reinforcements and punishments that we give people at work. In other words, we end up punishing the behaviors we want from people and reinforcing the behaviors we do not want. Two classic examples of this reversal follow.

A person learns to do an important task that no one else in the organization can perform anywhere near her level of competence. This task is an integral part of a complicated project, and completion of this task becomes vital to the success of this equally important project. Because of this person's ability, she is assigned to every project that involves completion of this task. The result is a tremendous work overload heaped upon this individual, requiring her to work constantly to meet all the demands for her services. We could conclude that this is not a desirable situation for this person and that learning this task has now become a punishing experience for her. Is this what the organization had in mind when the person was trained for this special task? Probably not. The intention was more likely to provide this person with new skills that would add value to both herself and the organization. All of this was intended to be reinforcement, not punishment. But this was not the way things turned out to be. Do you think this individual would be receptive to being trained in some future special skill that would result in it completely dominating her job? Probably not.

The corollary to this story is the worker who has an absentee problem. Many disciplinary programs progress through a series of increasingly severe punishments for continued violation of the rules, such as repeated absences. Often, particularly for an hourly workforce, these steps include a suspension from work for a specified period of time. When an absenteeism problem continues to this level of discipline, the rules might dictate that a suspension from work is appropriate. Think about what is happening in this circumstance. The person has a problem reporting to work regularly. The punishment is a suspension, giving the person more time off. In this case the punishment might be more of a reinforcement than a punishment.

The point is that we need to be conscious of what the actual effects are of the actions we take. You need to make certain that you are not punishing desired performance and reinforcing undesirable performance. As these examples illustrate, this is not so easy to keep straight!

A point that also needs to be made in this discussion about reinforcements and punishments is that they can be different for everyone. In the first example, all the extra work involved in learning the new skill might have indeed been reinforcing to an individual. The person might have welcomed the increased visibility and development opportunities associated with the increased responsibilities. In the second example, the person's absenteeism leading up to the disciplinary suspension might have put him in a financial hardship. The suspension, presumably without pay, would only aggregate this situation, making it a very undesirable one for this individual. Like so many other things associated with giving performance feedback, both punishment and reinforcement can be as individualized as those who are part of the process.

How do these principles affect performance feedback? What do we focus on in our performance evaluations, and what effect does this ultimately have influencing people's performance both positively and negatively? Are we reinforcing those behaviors we want to strengthen or are we punishing them?

Looking at all of this in the context of the performance standards you hold people to at work, is performance feedback in your organization negatively based? Is the focus of the feedback people receive really on the 5 percent to 10 percent of their job performance they don't do perfectly? Are we really looking for positives in people's behavior or are we so conditioned to find something negative in everything we look at? Can we be satisfied with anything less than perfect performance? Do we see the glass half empty or half full? Or are we constantly looking for a water fountain?

As discussed, most people perform the vast majority of the functions of their jobs correctly or even to perfection in many cases. A pie chart depicting the percent of job done correctly is in Figure 9-a. If you supervise others, fill in the pie chart in Figure 9-b by showing what percent of your subordinates' jobs are generally performed correctly. If you don't supervise others, use your own performance as an example.

Figure 9-a. Example of Percent of Job
Your Subordinates Do Correctly

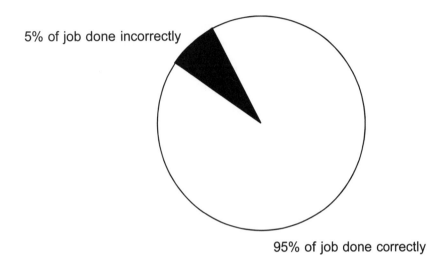

5% of job done incorrectly

95% of job done correctly

Figure 9-b. Percent of Job Your
Subordinates Do Correctly

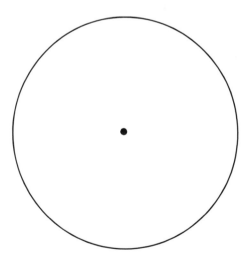

Now look at the percentage of "incorrect performance" you charted in Figure 9-b. What makes up the vast majority of your subordinates' performance concerning what they do correctly or what they do incorrectly? What do you focus on most concerning your feedback performance? Do you tend to take for granted what people do correctly on their jobs and not adequately reinforce this behavior? Do you seem to gravitate too easily to the negative aspects of people's performance? What are some examples?

_____

_____

_____

_____

_____

_____

Think back to the last performance appraisals you gave to your subordinates (or that you received). Was there a fair balance of positives and negatives presented? In other words, was the amount of time or emphasis that was spent on the negative aspects of the overall job performance commensurate with the percentage of incorrect performance you charted in Figure 9-b?

Stated another way, if an employee performed his or her job 95 percent correctly, does 95 percent of this person's performance appraisal consist of recognition of correct job performance? Is 95 percent of the time spent reviewing the person's performance centered on these positive aspects? Again, the questions become: Are you reinforcing the positive aspects of people's job performance centered on these positive aspects? Are you reinforcing the positive aspects of people's job performance adequately enough to strengthen these behaviors? Or are you focused on punishing poor performance?

Ultimately, the answers to these important questions lie with the person receiving the feedback. How the individual feels about the feedback he or she receives concerning their performance is the ultimate test. Oversimplified, there is a bias on the part of the subordinate to want to focus on the positive aspects of their job performance. Everyone, if given a choice, would rather hear positive things about themselves than negative. If a supervisor has a negative focus concerning performance in general, there is less chance that the feedback will meet all of its objectives.

Figure 10. Negative vs. Positive Performance Focus

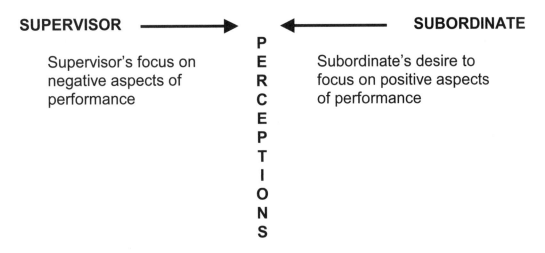

These different perceptual focuses on the positive versus the negative aspects of performance can significantly diminish the effectiveness of the entire performance feedback process.

These perceptions can also have a distorting effect on what actually transpires during a performance appraisal session. Feedback not necessarily intended to be negative or critical often becomes misinterpreted. Once sensitized, an individual might take virtually everything presented as being an attack on his or her performance record. Many of the performance rating systems that are used today feed this syndrome. Because these systems are by design very conservative in assigning the highest rating classifications, the vast majority of people fall into the middle category. To many people, this is a message that they are only average or "C-level" performers.

Many people react negatively to being described in this way. It might be contrary to their personal performance standards and work ethics. The very reasons that they might have reached their present position might be due to their ability to excel beyond the average or norm. They might be working harder than they ever have in their entire lives in their present jobs, and all the recognition they get is what is perceived by them as an average rating. All this frustration on the part of the employee occurs despite the supervisor's repeated assurances that their performance is perfectly acceptable and no reason to be upset. Yea right, here comes another KA-BOOM!

This phenomenon is further exaggerated by the person's perceptions relative to the proportion of time spent actually dealing with any areas of their performance that needs to be improved. Even if the actual amount of time spent on these negative factors is proportionally correct in relation to the overall presentation of feedback, their personal perceptions might again seem quite different.

This last point brings to mind something Albert Einstein once said concerning relativity. If a man places his hand on a hot stove, his perception of the passage of time will be relatively slow. However, during the same amount of time, a man was in the presence of a beautiful woman, and the passage of time was much faster. Everything is indeed relative to what you are experiencing concerning the passage of time it takes to complete any task.

Self-Concepts

People have certain self-concepts they need to protect during the performance appraisal and feedback process. These self-concepts might be threatened as a result of being evaluated and will also cause many perceptual barriers to be created. A supervisor needs to know and understand the person they are evaluating and have some idea about what their self-concepts might be that need to be protected.

Knowingly or unknowingly attacking these self-concepts will only cause even stronger perceptual barriers to exist. These perceptual barriers might cause the person to rationalize this feedback as being unrelated to his or her actual performance. There becomes a "disconnect" between how an individual perceives his or her self and their perceptions of how they see their own job performance. These differences can cause many rationalizations to occur concerning a person's job performance. This might begin as frustration and lead to a situation where the person is resentful toward their supervisor.

These emotions will present themselves in many ways and be played out in different forms. An employee might display "brooding" behavior or contribute at a very low level just within the bottom of the spectrum of acceptable job performance. When minimally performing his or her job, a person might rationalize, "Why should I break my back over this job if no one ever appreciates what I do anyway?" These silent (and sometimes not so silent) protests that people take on at work are probably the greatest source of lost productivity and inefficiencies in business today.

If you are not convinced of the magnitude of this problem, just listen to what people talk about at work. Most of the time (unless you are the boss), you hear people complaining to each other about something relating to work. Most likely they will share with one another examples of injustices that have occurred to them that they didn't deserve. Often, it is the boss who is the "villain" of the story who just doesn't appreciate the extra efforts and ability of the person. As co-workers empathize with one another's frustrations at work, they provide valuable support systems for themselves. The potential of these supportive peer relationships will be discussed later on in this book when we talk more about the advantages of peer feedback systems. For now, it should suffice to say that it is not difficult to find people venting these types of frustrations to one another in virtually any work setting. The real question is not "What is the magnitude of this problem?" but rather "Is there anything that can possibly be done to improve it?"

Before we leave the subject of the consequences of performance feedback, a few more points about negative feedback need to be made. It can be argued that negative feedback is a critically important aspect of performance feedback. If people are going to experience job growth and development, then they must address the weaker areas of their job performance. Obviously, the only way they can work on these aspects of their performance is if they are made aware of their weaknesses. The question is not if these communications should take place, but rather how. A good analogy again from the field of medicine is that "You don't want to cure the disease and kill the patient in the process!" It is important to always keep in mind that the ultimate goal of performance feedback is to help the individual improve their job performance, not to shoot them down. Negative feedback should be given in a constructive manner and not in a mean-spirited way.

Often, as part of the performance feedback process, a supervisor might ask his or her subordinates for feedback about his or her own performance. These same principles concerning negative feedback still need to apply. Just because one is in a supervisory role doesn't make him or her less sensitive, contrary to popular opinion. A subordinate shouldn't look at this as a unique opportunity to "get even" with their supervisor. This upward feedback needs to be constructive and not malicious or mean. It needs to precisely describe what aspects of the supervisor's performance creates problems for the subordinate and what might be done to improve this situation. The person giving this feedback needs to commit to being supportive in helping the other person improve and commit to continuing further dialog on this subject. Finally, everyone needs to keep an open mind about the feedback that was given and accept it in the spirit in which it was intended.

Everyone needs to be responsible for the feedback they give to one another. You can't just give someone feedback and then leave that person "hanging." After giving feedback, you need to provide support, follow up to help the other person deal with the feedback, and develop an improvement plan. In addition, feedback must be given for the right reasons and not be hurtful and mean. It should not be given simply to serve a personal agenda of the individual providing it.

A question that needs to be continuously repeated in any discussion about performance feedback is "What is the goal?" There is only one acceptable answer—to improve performance. We need to be constantly measuring our performance feedback efforts against this standard of performance. If any aspect of a performance feedback system does not support this objective, then it does not belong in the process. The same should be said about negative feedback. The ultimate test of its usefulness and appropriateness is if it somehow helps improve a person's performance. Sometimes we need to take a hard and introspective look at the true motivations of this type of feedback. We need to be sure that it really is constructive, not vindictive. It needs to be in the best interest of the receiver rather than of the giver of this feedback.

Case Study

John's boss rarely gave him any meaningful feedback about his performance. Typically, the only information he ever received on this subject was during his annual performance review. Even then, it seemed as if he could easily predict exactly what would be said and how he would be rated. His performance reviews had become a routine yearly exercise that had little meaning to either he or his supervisor. Truthfully, the review was conducted each year only because the organization required it in its standard procedures. Once signed off by John and his supervisor, the performance review was given little thought again until next year's requirement had to be met.

The problem with this situation was that there were certain aspects of John's performance that needed to be discussed that this process did not address. This caused problems not only for John, but for others who interacted with him as well. A number of John's job responsibilities were neither clearly defined or understood. No one was sure who was account-able for a number of these responsibilities, although many people thought they belonged to John. Everyone, including John, wished his supervisor would clarify what was expected of everyone concerning the scope of their jobs and responsibilities.

Because John's job responsibilities were not clearly defined in per-formance reviews, it was almost as if John and his supervisor had different ideas as to what his job involved. It seemed John saw his job as ABC, and his supervisor saw it as BCD.

John's perception of the job:

A_____ B_____ C_____

John's supervisor's perception of the job:

B_____ C_____ D_____

There were some overlaps between John's perception and his supervisor's perception of the job, but many discrepancies also existed. It was these perceptual differences that caused John's performance to be a source of frustration to both of them. John's annual performance review seemed to focus only on the "B" and "C" aspects of John's performance and did not address either "A" or "D."

Consequently, the supervisor always left these sessions feeling there were many areas of John's responsibilities that were not met, and John always felt that much of what he did was not being recognized by his supervisor.

Form vs. Process

Often, when an organization believes that improvements need to be made in their performance feedback process, the first thing they look at is the form that is currently being used to document performance appraisals. As discussed in Chapter 6, Levels of Performance Feedback, it is important to have a formal document to record what takes place during performance appraisal sessions. However, caution needs to be taken to ensure that the form itself doesn't become the entire performance feedback process. No matter how excellent the design of the performance appraisal form, it is nothing more than a tool that is used in the process. The emphasis needs to be on the goals, standards, commitments, philosophy, support, resources, sincerity, etc., that are all part of the entire performance feedback process. Focusing only on the design of the performance appraisal form can take away from the relative importance of these other factors.

This is not to say that the form's design is not important; the performance appraisal form can have the potential of providing direction and guidance toward achieving both personal and organizational goals. The point is that the form is not the entire process. Simply improving its design will probably not significantly improve performance feedback in your organization without examining the entire feedback process.

The number of performance-rating categories used in a performance feedback and appraisal process can be both an important and sometimes controversial subject. There can be problems with having both too many rating categories as well as too few. Having too many can cause performance feedback to be not specific enough. For example, say a performance feedback system comprises six categories:

- Disciplinary
- Unacceptable
- Needing Improvement
- Acceptable
- Above Expectations
- Excellent

One might ask, "What is the difference between the Disciplinary, Unacceptable, and Needing Improvement categories? Aren't they all essentially saying the same thing about the person's job performance—that there is a problem that needs to be addressed? Similarly, what is gained by having both the performance-rating categories of Above Expectations and Excellent? Aren't they both describing performance that is beyond what is required of the person?"

On the other hand, having too few categories can also create other problems. Many performance rating systems have been reduced to no more than three or four categories. People might feel that this number of categories is not enough to accurately make the distinctions necessary to describe people's true performance. For instance a typical three-level performance-rating system might have categories similar to the following:

- Poor
- Acceptable
- Superior

Having fewer rating categories might eliminate the confusion that a larger number would create, but will place the majority of people into a single category. This is illustrated in Figure 11, showing how a normal bell-shaped distribution curve results from having only three performance-rating categories.

Figure 11. Example of a Three Performance-Rating Category System with a Bell-Shaped Distribution

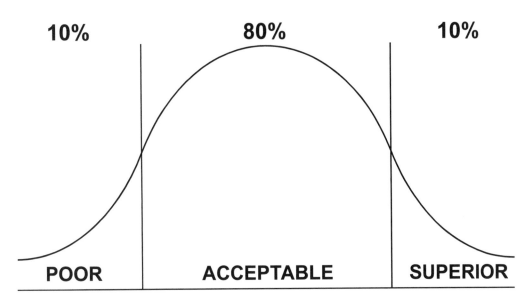

Assuming a normal bell-shaped distribution, this would result in approximately 80 percent of the people in an organization falling into the Acceptable level of performance, with the remaining 20 percent in the other two extremes. This same distribution can be found in virtually any measure of human performance or characteristics. The problem again is people's self-perceptions. Even though statistically most people's performance might fall into this middle category, their self-perceptions might be very different. Labeling as simply "average" the majority of people who work hard day in and day out to meet the increasing demands of their jobs might not create a very motivating work environment for them.

Chapter 6

Levels of Performance Feedback

This chapter will review the levels of performance feedback and will put into context many of the different ways people can receive this type of information. This is not necessarily intended to be a continuum of bad to good concerning which is the best way to receive performance feedback, although receiving no feedback certainly would be the most undesirable situation of any presented. The most important factor in evaluating any of these various levels of performance feedback is what is most appropriate for the organization. The organization must be able to support the feedback methodologies that are put in place and practiced. The necessary skill training must be provided as well as the time to implement the process. Each level requires various amounts of involvement and commitment on the part of different people in the organization. Obviously, the more complex levels will require more time and resources to implement than having no formal or documented feedback system in place.

For any performance feedback system to be effective, it must be implemented. Although this might sound rather redundant to say, this point can be critical. If a performance feedback system is not consistently implemented, it will lose its effectiveness and even credibility. There is typically a natural inclination for people to feel uncomfortable not only receiving feedback about their performance but also providing it. Without the support of management and, perhaps more important, their insistence, most performance feedback processes would cease to exist.

There can be a thousand and one excuses why managers or supervisors didn't have the time or resources available to give employees feedback on their job performance. The busy work schedules of managers and supervisors today make it difficult to make time to provide performance feedback, and it is often equally hard to free up employees to participate in the process as well. With the flattening of organizations, supervisors have more employees reporting to them. The shear number of people they must appraise combined with increased work loads and responsibilities can make providing performance feedback to employees seem like an impossible task. Conducting performance appraisals might fall lower and lower on a manager's or supervisor's priority list as pressures increase to get more and more work out with fewer resources. Even if conducted, performance appraisals that were once meaningful can now become nothing more than a ritual that must be held to meet the minimal requirements of the organization.

It is important to remember that other systems are often linked to performance feedback. Some of these interrelated systems ensure the completion of the performance feedback and appraisal process. For instance, in a merit-based performance system, the entire compensation process is dependent on the performance rating of employees. If there were no performance feedback evaluations given, there would be no basis for the distribution of compensation.

There are arguments both pro and con about the advantages of tying together performance feedback and compensation systems. Linking performance feedback to other systems, thus ensuring its completion, is certainly one of the most compelling reasons. There are other motivational factors that must be considered. In systems in which pay and performance are not linked, such as the case in many hourly workforce compensation systems, there might seem to be little reason to improve performance on the job. No matter how hard you work, your pay will be no different than the person next to you who puts forth only a minimal effort. Yet, in virtually every such work environment, there are employees who do take enormous amounts of pride in their job and performance. Conversely, there are those who work in a merit-based performance system who show no evidence of motivation in their jobs.

The issue of linking performance to pay is a complex one. Obviously, it is influenced by many factors. Transcending all of these arguments both for or against merit systems is the fact that people need to receive feedback about their job performance. As you will see as we review the various levels of performance feedback, a number of these formats may or may not lend themselves to being connected to personnel or compensation systems. This discussion, at least for now, is presented independent of whether a performance merit system is in place or not. The focus here is primarily on how people receive performance feedback independent of linkage to compensation, but recognizing its potential influence on this process.

The remainder of this chapter will focus on the following outline of the various levels of performance feedback that might exist in an organization. These levels describe different approaches as well as philosophies of providing performance feedback. Keep in mind that there are no absolutes concerning performance feedback approaches. In other words, there are probably "pockets" of each of these levels to be found in many or most organizations. These levels are identified to bring awareness to these tendencies and orientations that organizations gravitate to in their approaches to providing performance feedback.

Again, it is the execution of the performance feedback system or process more than methodology that will ultimately determine its effectiveness.

Levels of Performance Feedback

There are six levels of performance feedback:

I. No feedback

II. No formal feedback or documentation

III. Formal feedback system including written documentation, but no personalized communications

IV. Formal feedback system including personalized communications from supervisor to supervisor

V. Formal system, multi-source

VI. Self-directed feedback (discussed in Chapter 7)

Skill-Building Questions

At which of these levels do you see your organization providing performance feedback?

_____

_____

_____

_____

_____

_____

Compare how you answered the previous question at this time in your organization to what level you would like to receive performance feedback in the future.

_____

_____

_____

_____

_____

_____

Level I. No Feedback

You might think it would be rare for a work environment to exist in which there is no feedback to employees about their performance. However, it is probably more prevalent than you might imagine. It can even exist in a merit-based performance system. In this situation, merit raises are arbitrarily assigned by someone or even a group and sent directly to payroll with no explanation to those receiving them each year. The only positive aspect of this type of system is that it is easier for managers and supervisors to implement. Not only do most people dislike receiving performance feedback, supervisors do not relish the thought of giving it.

As might be expected, non-merit systems have an even greater likelihood of providing no feedback to employees. Because there are probably no other formal systems directly connected to it, the absence of formal feedback does not interfere with other personnel-related functions. An organization will typically "slip" into a no-feedback mode, rather than intentionally instituting one, if no other systems are affected.

It has become common for organizations that at one time had a well-developed performance feedback program for employees to no longer see this function as a priority. Due to either downsizing or reorganizations, supervisors' and managers' responsibilities have greatly increased. As they began to prioritize the things they realistically could and could not accomplish, providing performance feedback sank to the bottom of the list.

At first, all the rationale for not providing feedback to employees sounded legitimate. In many of these situations, supervisors might have been reassigned to new areas or might have newly combined areas of responsibility. The number of direct reports for which the supervisor is now responsible might have grown immensely. It would be completely understandable that the supervisor under these new circumstances would not be able to provide meaningful feedback to new subordinates right away. In these circumstances, there are certainly many other pressing issues and priorities that must be attended to first. You won't shut down the organization's operations by not providing feedback to employees. It is very doubtful that customers would even know or care if feedback was provided to employees. In fact, it might be a long time before anyone even realized that performance feedback was no longer being given. Keeping in mind that giving and receiving performance feedback is not exactly high on most people's favorite things to do, there would probably not be too many complaints about its absence.

This scenario can leave a real void in the feedback communications in an organization. The system was originally designed to include a performance feedback program for employees. It probably was the single source for employees to receive feedback from anyone in the organization. Now that it has been allowed to no longer exist, there are no other performance feedback systems to back it up.

Regardless of how this lack of performance feedback came to exist, employees working in this environment can only guess how their supervisor feels about their job performance. Obviously, a total absence of feedback is probably unlikely. Employees are most likely told when they do something wrong, thus once again validating the age-old performance feedback adage, "If you don't hear anything, you are doing just fine, but...." You know the rest of this by now!

There is a story that could be told in many workplaces about an employee who was unexpectedly "summoned" into his boss's office one day. As he walked to the boss's office, he searched his memory for what he must have done wrong for such an unusual meeting to be arranged. "It must have been those numbers on the Green project that I didn't have time to double check," he thought to himself as he continued what seemed to be an endless trek to the boss's office. "No, now that I think about it, I did verify those numbers. I know that they were all correct. Then what is it? I must be getting out! Yea, that's what it must be. The only other time I have been invited to the boss's office was when I was hired," he decided as he knocked on the heavy wooden door and was told to enter what he was sure was to be his job's execution chamber. Bravely, he stood before the boss's large mahogany desk inside the office awaiting his "sentencing."

"Sit down, Smith," the boss ordered in a somewhat cheerful tone unfitting the painful business that Smith was now convinced was about to take place.

"He's probably just trying to soften me up for the kill," he thought to himself. The possibility of an attractive severance package was beginning to occur to him.

"How long have you been with us now, Smith?" the boss asked once Smith had settled as comfortably as he could in one of the overstuffed leather chairs in front of the mahogany desk.

"A little over five years," Smith meekly answered.

"Hmmm…, it's been that long already?" the boss said looking very pensive and thoughtful.

"Boy, he's really dragging this thing out," Smith thought. "Why doesn't he just do it and get this over with!"

"Smith, we've been very impressed with your work over these past five years," the boss began to say.

"I just know what's coming next," Smith assured himself. "He's going to tell me what a shame it is to have to let me go and how difficult a decision this was to make."

"Talented people like you are not easily found. We're very lucky to have you on our team. That's why I would like to offer you a promotion to Section Manager. What do you say, Smith? Do you want the job?" the boss asked.

"Well Sir, I really don't know what to say," Smith stammered out, shocked by the promotion he had just received. "Thank you and I won't let you down," he heard himself promising as the boss was shaking his hand in congratulations and walking him to the door, anxious to get on with the next business he had to attend to.

Although this scene might have been a bit dramatized to make its point, it is undoubtedly a familiar one for many people. It is not that unusual for someone to not know with any degree of certainty whether he or she is going to be fired or promoted at any given time in their career.

This situation definitely worsens in those work environments in which there is no feedback system of any kind in place.

Besides the many personal problems this lack of communication causes people who must work in these systems, there can be legal implications as well. These problems can be troublesome for both the employer as well as the employee. Without any discussions, records, or documentation concerning people's job performance, the organization might not be in a very defensible position concerning its employment and personnel actions. This can be impacted by the broad spectrum of potential legal liabilities that organizations face today including Equal Opportunities, Affirmative Action, and the Americans with Disabilities Act.

Perhaps most importantly, without any feedback, people have far fewer opportunities to grow professionally in their jobs. Supervisors might be constantly dissatisfied with certain aspects of their subordinates' job performance that never get addressed and instead are allowed to continue with no corrective action ever to take place.

Level II. No Formal Feedback or Documentation

More likely than the scenario presented in the previous section is the existence in an organization of some form of performance feedback even though it might not be formal or documented. Not being formal or documented means there is no official system in place that requires or even regulates the performance feedback process. There are no standardized forms that are used nor any other written records of performance appraisals of feedback. Performance feedback is not tied to other personnel systems in any formal way. Without a formalized feedback system in place, there can be no direct connection to promotions, salary increases, career development, demotions, terminations, personal growth, or any other opportunities.

One must wonder how in the absence of a formalized feedback system an organization can function. Curiously, the lack of a formalized feedback system does not preclude the existence of personnel functions. Employees still get promoted, receive raises, are given developmental experiences, and are demoted or even terminated due to performance all without a formal performance feedback system in place. There undoubtedly must be a lot of surprises in a system such as this!

Working in this type of feedback environment, people are probably much more likely to be told when they do something wrong than be given positive feedback about their performance. But how do people know where they stand concerning promotions, raises, demotions, development, and those other important events in their careers without any feedback?

The answer in this case is that all communications concerning any of these career-related topics are informal without any supporting documentation. These communications might indeed take place, but probably not on a regular or predictable schedule. There is no interrelation between any systems that support people's career development in the organization. There is no database for the organization to tap into for candidate searches for positions that need to be filled. This can be even more of a problem for those openings that might need a very specific set of qualifications or are difficult to fill for other various reasons. Lack of this data is a lose-lose situation for both the organization and the employees; they both miss out on opportunities because of it.

The lack of formal or documented performance feedback will ultimately result in everyone being confused about where they stand in the organization. The system for giving promotions might be perceived as one of favoritism. In reality, without having at least some kind of objective criteria for evaluating people's performance, what other system could exist? If merit raises are not tied to a formal evaluation process, how can they be distributed in a fair and objective manner? Aggravating these perceptions of unfairness and favoritism in a system such as this is the likelihood that all or most of these decisions will be made by one individual: the boss.

If the boss likes you, then your career will go along very smoothly, regardless of how you perform your job. If the boss doesn't like you, well—KA-BOOM!

This can certainly be a very frustrating and demotivating environment for people to work in. The organization itself suffers as well by not having the ability to properly identify and reward those who are truly the top performers. What is really concerning is just how prevalent this type of feedback system might be in organizations today. Although probably less likely in larger organizations, this "If you don't hear anything…" approach to performance feedback can easily become the default performance feedback system.

All this can lead to performance feedback becoming a high priority only when there is a problem that has to be addressed. Resolution to the problem usually means "lining up the guilty parties and shooting them at dawn." When performance feedback becomes exclusively punitive based, it is unlikely that it is developmental in any way. Proactive initiatives to prevent problems from recurring are not put into place. People involved have limited growth opportunities from these types of experiences. They probably invest their energies instead in trying to ensure that they never find themselves in this situation again in the future.

Obviously, there are many problems with not having a formal documented performance feedback system. People's developmental needs are not as readily apparent to those who can have a positive impact upon them. Organizations lose their objectivity in the development of their people. Everyone, particularly the employees, can become confused and sometimes very frustrated by not knowing exactly how their performance is perceived by their boss as well as by others in the organization.

Case Study

An example of the problems that a system such as this can create is illustrated in the following case study example:

"Who's going to replace Mary Sullivan when she takes that big job in the corporate office?" was the question on everyone's mind in the organization. Mary was District Sales Manager for the most successful region in the company. She had broken record after record for her performance, and now she was getting her well-earned reward—a promotion to Vice President of Sales and Marketing. When the position became open due to a retirement, there was little doubt in anyone's mind who was the most qualified candidate for the job. You really didn't have to have a formal performance feedback system or management development process in place to figure out who should get this important job. Everyone agreed it belonged to Mary.

However, other positions are not always quite so easy to find the best candidates for consideration. For instance, there were a number of potential candidates for Mary's old position. One of her first assignments as VP was to select who should succeed her as District Sales Manager. Unfortunately for her, the company did not have a formal performance feedback system in place. There had been a program years ago, but with all the downsizing that had occurred over the past few years and the increased workloads of everyone, it had been allowed to fall along the wayside.

Although Mary knew the candidates who had worked for her when she was the District Sales Manager, she did not know any others who were under consideration. She was surprised to learn that the other candidates had not received any formal or documented performance feedback in more than five years. When she asked for what ever documentation might exist for the potential candidates for her old job, she was given paperwork on only two of the seven candidates, and they had both worked for her!

How was she going to objectively consider the other five candidates? If she were to select one of the people who had worked for her, it might appear to be favoritism. However, she had no basis to make a decision on the other candidates except "word of mouth." "What criteria can I use to make the best decision about who I should select for this job?" she wondered as she looked the list of potential candidates over and over again.

Skill-Building Questions

What candidate(s) do you think Mary gave the most serious consideration to and why?

_____

_____

_____

_____

What are the problems with not having a formal documented performance feedback system in place?

_____

_____

_____

_____

What do you think the reaction might be from others in the organization concerning who you believe Mary will select for this position?

_____

_____

_____

_____

Skill-Building Questions (continued)

What would you do concerning this problem if you were Mary?

_____

_____

_____

_____

Level III. Formal Feedback System

There are many variations of formal feedback systems that include documentation, but not personalized communications. At first, you might wonder how people can receive performance feedback about themselves without it being personalized. Not being personalized means the information is of a more quantitative nature rather than narrative. The quantitative approach of performance feedback might be in the form of a rating scale. Performance feedback is received via a series of indexed ratings to describe the person's performance against an established standard or criteria.

This type of performance feedback format is perhaps the most common. In many ways, it is probably also the easiest to complete for the evaluator. It is similar to filling out a questionnaire about another person in which you select from a list of multiple choices. This approach to performance feedback does not typically address any specific or personalized aspects of the individual's behaviors or results at work. It relies almost entirely on the information provided on the evaluation form as the set of behaviors to evaluate the person. There might be a section at the end of the evaluation form for the supervisor to write a few brief personalized remarks, but this is not the main emphasis of this format. Because of the impersonalized focus of this evaluation form, these comments might be very general in nature and do not address any substantive performance areas or issues. They are by design usually only summary statements to bring closure to the quantitative feedback just presented.

However, it is interesting to note how much more of an impact these brief statements can have than the previous pages of quantitative measures if they provide true insights into how the supervisor feels about the person's performance. This is not to say that the quantitative approach to performance feedback is not useful. First and foremost it does provide formal feedback to the individual and can address a great number of performance areas in a concise manner. Because of its quantitative design, comparisons in performance can be easily made from one evaluation period to another.

By providing set criteria, this approach can be a consistent way to deliver performance feedback. In effect, the performance evaluation form becomes a checklist of performance criteria to be reviewed for each person. This format might be preferred by many supervisors because of its straightforward approach. In many of the various designs of this format, there are certain formulas that are part of the completion process of the form. As a result, there is often an accompanying performance index scale that assigns a rating based on the resulting points assigned to each performance rating area.

A brief example of a quantitative feedback format is shown on the following page, along with the rating and scoring criteria.

Quantitative Feedback Example

Ratings: 1 = Poor   2 = Good   3 = Excellent

	Rating	**Importance**	**Value**

Meets deadlines and completes assignments on time.   _____ x _____ = _____

Shows initiative on the job. Does more than required.   _____ x _____ = _____

Has technical knowledge and skills required for the job.   _____ x _____ = _____

Communicates clearly both in writing and speaking.   _____ x _____ = _____

Is cooperative and displays positive attitude.   _____ x _____ = _____

Scoring:

Add the Ratings column: _____

Add the Value column: _____

Divide the Value column by the Ratings column to determine overall performance rating: Performance Rating: _____

General Comments: _____

_____

_____

Although there is some subjectiveness to how an individual's scores might have been arrived upon, the rest of the evaluation progress is in a very formatted manner. A rating can be easily analyzed and broken down into the person's strengths and weaknesses that contributed to their final score. A weighting system such as the one shown in the example takes into account the various requirements of the different jobs that will be evaluated using this form. Particular tasks given a high degree of importance might be highlighted as being more significant on the person's overall evaluation.

This format also offers the advantage of providing the evaluator with all the performance criteria that is to be rated. This set format eliminates the need for the evaluator to identify and describe the elements of the person's specific job that is to be rated. This pre-established criteria is much less personal than one that specifically includes references to the job that is being evaluated.

This approach does offer certain benefits and advantages over more personalized formats. The most obvious is that these performance evaluation forms are easier and less time consuming to complete. This can be a very important factor for busy supervisors today who have many people to evaluate.

In many ways, this set format might pose less of a threat to both the supervisor and the person being evaluated. Because it is less personal, there is not as great a potential threat to a person's self-esteem. The focus of the entire evaluation might be more on the "bottom line" numerical rating than on any of the specific details of the evaluation. This format is typically relatively brief in length and can be reviewed with the recipient in less time than many of the approaches to be discussed.

Level IV. Formal Feedback System— Personalized Communications

This format typically combines numerical or quantitative performance measures and personalized feedback. The performance feedback form is designed so that the supervisor is required to personalize certain aspects of the feedback that the individual will receive. This might involve referring to the individual's specific job responsibilities as the focus of the performance to be reviewed. This makes the performance feedback more personalized and specific to the person being evaluated. There might also be pre-established descriptions of generalized performance criteria similar to those described in the previous section. The combination of these two approaches allows for some degree of consistency in the measure that each person is evaluated against as well as the flexibility to recognize differences in the responsibilities of jobs. This flexibility is particularly important for more complex and higher-level positions. It would be unfair to the people in these positions not to have a standard way of recognizing the unique characteristics of these jobs in the performance evaluation methods.

The more personalized the performance feedback becomes, the more meaning it can have for the individual receiving it. Nothing is more upsetting to an individual being evaluated than to perceive that their supervisor does not really have an adequate understanding of their job performance. The more personalized and specific the supervisor can make the feedback presented, the more likely the person will be receptive to the input. The ultimate goal of any performance feedback initiative must be first to have the recipient understand and accept the information about his or her performance. If a person for any reason does not believe in the reliability or validity of the feedback, it will have little or no benefit. This again begins the scenario of a "performance feedback trial" in which the subordinate is the defendant and the supervisor is the prosecuting attorney. The performance feedback session becomes more of a case against the employee presented by his or her supervisor who tries to justify why the employee received the rating he or she did.

An important component of this type of performance feedback is the follow-up action plans that might be part of its overall design. Even more important than an individual's past performance is what their performance will be in the future. Again, this must be the overall objective of any performance feedback approach. It is very important that there be acceptance of any future developmental plans for improved or even sustained performance. The more input a person has in developing these objectives, the more likely he or she will accept and work toward meeting them in the future.

An example of this type of performance feedback combining both personalized and pre-established criteria is shown below:

Key:

1 = Developmental Need   3 = Highly Effective
2 = Acceptable Performance   4 = Top Performance

SECTION A:
JOB ACCOUNTABILITIES
(Based on Job Description)

	1	2	3	4
A. _____	_____	_____	_____	_____
B. _____	_____	_____	_____	_____
C. _____	_____	_____	_____	_____
D. _____	_____	_____	_____	_____
E. _____	_____	_____	_____	_____
F. _____	_____	_____	_____	_____

SECTION B: OVERALL PERFORMANCE ACCOUNTABILITIES

OVERALL PERFORMANCE ACCOUNTABILITIES	1	2	3	4
1. **Communications**—Interacts positively with co-workers on all levels of the organization.	____	____	____	____
2. **Organization Skills**—Meets deadlines and commitments. Is able to store and retrieve information in an efficient manner.	____	____	____	____
3. **Innovation/Creativity**—Finds different ways to solve problems. Is resourceful in finding answers to difficult problems.	____	____	____	____
4. **Job Skills**—Has the necessary skills to perform the job. If deficient in any area(s), develops a plan to improve necessary skills.	____	____	____	____
5. **Commitment**—Is dedicated to performing job to the best of his/her ability. Works toward continuously improving performance.	____	____	____	____

Level V. Formal System, Multi-Source

In each of the previous levels of performance feedback, there has been at least one common factor: The supervisor has been the source of the performance feedback. Even though in most circumstances the supervisor would likely seek input from others in the organization, he or she is still the focal point for providing this information to the individual.

In this level of performance feedback, the focus begins to change from a single source (supervisor) to a multiple source.

Multiple-source performance feedback provides an individual a number of different perspectives about how others in the organization see him or her. This can be particularly valuable feedback for the individual because it eliminates many of the inherent problems of single-source feedback discussed earlier. For instance, biases that one might perceive their supervisor has against them can distract from any feedback received from their boss. "He just said that because he doesn't like me," someone might rationalize when presented with any areas for improvement during a performance review with their supervisor.

Multiple-source feedback eliminates, or perhaps at least minimizes, this perception. It is more difficult to deny the validity of constructive feedback when it is received from a number of sources, some of whom might even be peers and friends. This can be very powerful information that will if nothing else get the attention of those who receive it.

As mentioned, in the more traditional performance feedback systems, there are typically specific rating guidelines that force performance ratings to be distributed on a bell-shaped distribution curve. This limiting factor can influence the feedback that people receive. If the organization's allocation of top ratings has already been reached, others deserving of high ratings might be forced into lower performance rating categories. Consequently, their evaluation might be developed more to justify the lower rating than to accurately evaluate the individual's performance. Figure 12 illustrates the potentially limiting effect on performance feedback that rating distribution systems can create. Because this system allows only

25 percent of the entire employee population being evaluated to receive an "Excellent" rating, there might be a number of others who deserve the top ratings, but are denied because of these limitations. What effect does this have on the feedback they receive?

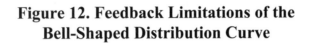

Figure 12. Feedback Limitations of the Bell-Shaped Distribution Curve

One of the major advantages of multiple-source feedback systems is that they pose no limitations on the amount of positive feedback people can receive. No one needs to feel that they have to justify their feedback or that they will be denying someone else in the organization by evaluating one person as "Excellent."

We will discuss two variations of multiple-source performance feedback systems that provide many advantages over traditional approaches: 360-degree feedback and team feedback.

360-Degree Feedback

This type of performance feedback has gained increasing popularity in the past several years. As the name implies, a person receives feedback from the "full circle" of other people who work around him or her. Feedback is provided by others from every direction including peers, subordinates, supervisors, and even the individual him- or herself. The idea is to give the individual personal feedback from a variety of perspectives to provide a more complete understanding of how others perceive him or her. This approach addresses many of the limitations described earlier in the discussion about "supervisor only" feedback systems. There are a number of training and development organizations and consultants who provide 360-degree feedback tools to customers. Their services include providing all the needed forms as well as analyzing the results and providing reports back to the participants.

When receiving performance feedback, one might dismiss the opinion of their supervisor as being biased against them and not a true reflection of their actual job performance. However, it is a much different story when the feedback comes from multiple sources including those other than your supervisor. 360-Degree feedback systems provide the individuals with feedback from a variety of levels in the organization. In a traditional supervisor-subordinate performance evaluation, the supervisor looks at a person's performance from an evaluative viewpoint. In 360-degree reviews, the purpose of the information is more from a feedback viewpoint. This is a very important distinction: The focus is on feedback rather than evaluation, taking this information out of the organization's formal evaluation process with all its implications on the person's career and future.

360-Degree feedback processes involve a standardized questionnaire that looks at a number of dimensions of an individual's job performance. Typically, forms are sent to a person's supervisor(s), peers, and direct reports, creating the full circle of feedback. There is also a form that the individual completes about his or her self-perceptions. Once sent in, the completed forms are summarized by the company who developed the feedback tool, and a confidential summary report is sent to the individual.

How are people typically viewed by those from various perspectives at work? Are their peers and direct reports more or less critical than their supervisor? How do people see themselves compared to these others? Of course, there are many different ways this data will result depending on the people involved. Figure 13, however, shows how 360-degree feedback often results.

Figure 13. 360-Degree Feedback Results

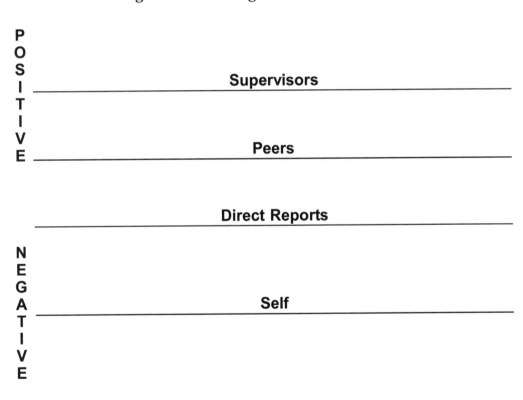

As can be seen, perhaps surprisingly, supervisors tend to provide the most positive feedback to individuals. A person's peers are typically a little less positive in their feedback than supervisors. Then direct reports tend to be somewhat critical, followed by the person's own self-perceptions, which tend to be the most negative. The fact that we are often our own worst critics is probably not a surprise to anyone.

Certainly there can be any number of variations of how an individual's job performance might be viewed by these various sources. These variations can sometimes provide the greatest insights. For example, let's say that a certain dimension of a person's job performance is rated by his or her supervisor as "fair," but everyone else in the study reported "excellent" ratings on this same dimension. What are some conclusions that the person might draw from this varied feedback? One such conclusion that needs to be considered is that the boss is seeing performance that no one else does. However, another viewpoint might be that the supervisor has misjudged the individual. The greater the variation between a single source of feedback and the majority opinion, the more likely that what is actually being revealed is not a true reflection of the person's ability, but something else affecting this different perception.

The feedback a person receives from a 360-degree study can provide an opportunity for an individual to take an honest and introspective look at himself or herself. They can identify both their strengths and weaknesses and develop action plans for both. With this information, an individual can go back to those who provided feedback and ask for their support in helping improve his or her performance. If the feedback indicates that there might be more of a relationship problem than a performance problem, goals to improve these situations can also be developed.

Again, the greatest advantage of this type of performance feedback (and team and self-directed feedback, to be discussed later) is that they typically are used as a developmental not evaluative tool. They are most effective when they are used on a non-consequential basis. In other words, a person should not feel that their future or career is "on the line" as a result of the feedback they receive. 360-Degree feedback is presented in a confidential manner, and the information is shared only if the person chooses to do so as part of their developmental plan.

Multiple-source feedback systems such as this also take into account the fact that we interact differently with different people. An individual might be a very effective supervisor, but might not be as good at being a subordinate, or vice versa. 360-Degree feedback gives a more accurate description of the person's total skill and performance capabilities. By better understanding how others see us, we can identify opportunities to continue to grow and improve our job performance.

Team Feedback

As organizations today are moving more toward teamwork and asking individuals to work closer together to reach shared goals, team feedback is becoming increasingly important.

This type of feedback tends to be less standardized and computerized. Typically an organization or team might develop their own form and format to meet their particular needs. The objective of team feedback systems needs to be focused on improving the effectiveness of the group. Teamwork is not something that always comes naturally to people. So much of our culture and learning experiences are focused on competition. Sports, academic grading systems, job selection, promotions, etc., are all based on the concept of competition. After years of being programmed to be the best you can to beat out the other guy, suddenly you find yourself being asked to work together for the good of the team. Is it really any wonder that people have difficulty embracing this concept?

Team feedback helps individuals focus on those aspects of their performance that are most supportive of the needs of the team and how they can make the greatest contributions. By providing this feedback to one another, team members are helping everyone work more effectively together. Often, there are aspects of an individual's job performance that he or she might not be aware of that are counter-productive to the team's goals. Sometimes, simply becoming aware of these problems is all that is needed to correct them. Other times, skills might need to be taught to help the person improve their team performance.

There are a number of decisions that need to be made concerning the "rules" for team feedback. A major decision is if the feedback should be anonymous or not. Typically, most people are more comfortable providing honest and candid feedback to team members if they are not identified as the source. This feedback should be shared only with the individual receiving it and not be provided to the team members, supervisor, or anyone else in the organization to ensure its confidentiality. Team members should be encouraged to follow up with peers to ask for their support in improving their team performance and contributions. Team meetings can be held to create overall developmental plans to improve the skills identified by the group as needing improvement.

A variation of team feedback is upward feedback programs. As mentioned in the discussion about self-concepts in Chapter 5, in this format, subordinates provide feedback to their supervisor in a similar way as they do to each other in 360-degree feedback. This might at first appear to be a role reversal of traditional feedback systems. However, this departure from the norm provides another opportunity for feedback rather than evaluation. It is equally important to ensure the confidentiality of the feedback that supervisors receive from those who work for them as it is with other sources of this information.

The challenge becomes how the organization can provide support to the team and its members by giving them the tools to work more effectively together. This support must be provided by addressing the needs identified by the team members themselves. Of course, the integrity and confidentiality of the team feedback must be maintained. At the same time, organizations must find acceptable ways to identify those skills that need to be provided to enable optimum team performance.

Some possible ways to make this information known include conducting surveys, needs assessments, team meetings, team developmental plans, committees, or focus groups. The main criterion is that there be efforts made to identify and address the development needs of the team that can be discovered through this process. There needs to be follow-up as an outcome of future team feedback to measure the effectiveness of these developmental efforts.

An example of a team feedback form is shown in Figure 14.

Figure 14. Team Feedback Form

Instructions: Please complete a team feedback form for each member of your team. All information will be kept confidential.

Team member's name: _____

Part I: Communications

A. **Listening:** Team member listens effectively to others. Gives others his/her full attention when listening. Avoids interrupting others. Strives to fully understand what other team members are saying.

1	2	3	4
Poor	**Fair**	**Good**	**Excellent**

Comments:

B. **Expressing Viewpoint:** Team member expresses him/herself in such a way that others understand the way he/she feels about various issues and topics at work.

1	2	3	4
Poor	**Fair**	**Good**	**Excellent**

Comments:

C. **Sharing Information:** Team member shares with others necessary information required to perform their jobs.

1	2	3	4
Poor	**Fair**	**Good**	**Excellent**

Comments:

Part II: Performance

A. **Job Skills:** Team member has acquired the skills necessary to perform his/her job effectively.

1	2	3	4
Poor	**Fair**	**Good**	**Excellent**

Comments:

B. **Commitment:** Team member puts forth the efforts necessary to perform his/her job effectively.

1	2	3	4
Poor	**Fair**	**Good**	**Excellent**

Comments:

C. **Quality:** Team member is committed to performing quality work that meets the requirements of the customer, both internal and external.

1	2	3	4
Poor	**Fair**	**Good**	**Excellent**

Comments:

Part III: Teamwork

A. **Team Player:** Team member works with the best interest of the team in mind.

1	2	3	4
Poor	**Fair**	**Good**	**Excellent**

Comments:

B. **Consensus:** Team member works to build consensus among the team. Will support the ideas of others even though he/she may not personally agree.

1	2	3	4
Poor	**Fair**	**Good**	**Excellent**

Comments:

C. **Win/Win:** Team member seeks win/win solutions to problems at work rather than win/lose. Works toward collaboration rather than competition.

1	2	3	4
Poor	**Fair**	**Good**	**Excellent**

Comments:

Part IV: Overall Feedback (optional)

Please provide the team member any additional feedback you would like to provide.

_____

_____

_____

_____

_____

_____

_____

_____

_____

_____

_____

_____

_____

_____

_____

_____

_____

_____

_____

In designing your own team feedback form, it might be best to keep it relatively simple and easy to complete in a short period of time. It is better to focus feedback on the dimensions of the job rather than on personal characteristics of the individual. Most likely, team members at least initially will not want to address the more sensitive issues of job performance, nor will they be receptive to being directly involved in disciplinary issues except in extreme cases. This is typically viewed as a management responsibility and not something that peers feel comfortable or prepared to address.

There are many ways that team feedback systems can be administered. E-mail, with its increasingly expanding use, can offer a very efficient way to send and receive performance feedback not previously available until recently.

The last level of performance feedback, self-directed feedback, will be reviewed in detail in the next chapter.

Chapter 7

Self-Directed Feedback

This chapter will review in detail the concept of self-directed feedback. Self-directed feedback, true to its name, places the control of performance feedback in the hands of the recipient. In each of the previous feedback systems discussed, there were pre-established guidelines to be followed in order to receive the information being sought. Self-directed feedback does not include such strict rigors or requirements. It seeks to change the paradigm of performance feedback from one of "bitter medicine" that must be endured to gain its benefits, to one of self-exploration that is seen as an opportunity for growth.

The concept of self-directed feedback recognizes the fact that people have different tolerances for feedback. Again, the medicine analogy is appropriate: Feedback must be given in the correct amounts and at the right time. The idea that "If a little of something is good, then a lot of it must be better" is no more true when it comes to feedback than with medicine. A correctly prescribed dose of medicine can cure a patient's disease; an overdose can kill the person or result in a bad side effect. The same medicine might not be appropriate for everyone even though their symptoms might appear to be similar. Usually a doctor will prescribe less powerful drugs to begin to find the cure to an illness. Progressively stronger medications and treatments might later be given as needed as the patient's tolerance increases to the drug. To begin a treatment regime too fast or aggressively can indeed "make the cure worse than the disease."

Self-directed feedback makes the individual the "feedback doctor." In other words, the person will prescribe for himself or herself how much or how little feedback they desire. Some people might want a great deal of feedback, while others might want relatively little. Self-directed feedback is customized to accommodate these differences. The main objective is to protect not only the messenger, but also the person receiving the message: Don't shoot the messenger or the receiver!

Self-directed feedback is intended to be non-evaluative in its design, similar to the 360-degree and team feedback systems. Self-directed feedback should also have no direct impact on other formal performance evaluation systems that are part of other compensation or organizational developmental processes. Self-directed feedback is intended to help the individual's personal development in such a manner that is most acceptable to himself or herself.

Going back to the feedback model presented in Chapter 3, perceptions both on the part of the sender and the receiver of feedback play an instrumental role in the ultimate message received. Self-directed feedback can be one of the best means of identifying and understanding these perceptual differences. The main goal of self-directed feedback is to explore the perceptions of others about an individual's performance. The objective is not only understanding these perceptions, but addressing them as well. Like many other aspects of interpersonal communication, awareness is the key to understanding.

Self-directed feedback is unique in that it begins from the point of view or perceptions of the receiver of feedback. In Figure 15, you can see that the feedback perspective this time begins with the receiver.

Figure 15. Self-Directed Feedback Perceptions

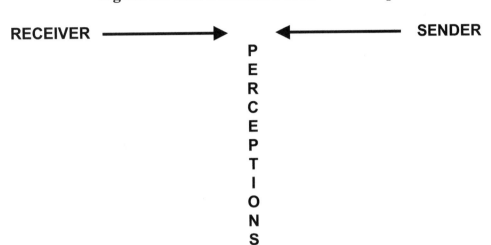

Although this at first seems like a subtle difference, it is important. In self-directed feedback, we are not just looking at perceptual differences in the way different people view performance, we are also beginning to address self-perceptions. Self-perceptions are the most important of all, and perhaps those that need the greatest care. Performance feedback can present a significant threat to an individual's self-perceptions. This is why most people if given the choice would probably opt not to receive feedback about their performance.

But what if feedback could be structured and designed so as not to pose such a threat to one's self-perceptions? Because the entire feedback process is in the control of the receiver, self-directed feedback has the potential of meeting this goal. Its principal advantage is the level of acceptance the individual will have concerning the feedback received. Instead of feedback becoming a potential threat to a person's self-perceptions, it is instead more of the learning opportunity it is intended to be.

To illustrate the benefits of self-directed feedback, let's first compare it to traditional performance feedback systems using the familiar five questions of Who? What? When? Where? and How?

Self-Directed Feedback Compared to Traditional Feedback

		TRADITIONAL	SELF-DIRECTED
WHO:	Who decides person(s) providing feedback?	Determined by system	Individual receiving feedback
WHAT:	What aspects of performance will be included in feedback?	Determined by the form/format	Individual designs own feedback criteria
WHEN:	When will feedback be given?	Schedule is set by the system	Individual sets own feedback schedule within certain parameters
WHERE:	Where does the feedback go after it is provided?	If part of the formal appraisal process, to the person's employment file	All information is in the control of the individual
HOW:	In what way is performance feedback administered?	According to established procedures	Individual develops own procedures

How Does Self-Directed Feedback Work?

Self-directed feedback begins with the premise that not everyone is able to accept and process performance feedback the same way. People have different tolerances for feedback. Some people can accept many different types of feedback from varying sources. Negative feedback might be viewed as an opportunity for one person and a personally threatening experience for another. This distaste for feedback might be the greatest perceptual barrier to overcome of all. There is in each of us at least some level of self-protection when it comes to feedback.

What is it about performance feedback that can be perceived as so threatening? What effect does this threat have on a person's future job performance? People often harbor many resentments as a result of negative feedback about their performance that they were not emotionally ready to receive. This can be the cause of poor job performance and strained working relationships. The biggest problem with this situation might be that those who are delivering this negative feedback believe that it accomplishes something positive. Instead it is probably aggravating a problem that has existed in a more dormant state. The very performance behavior that is attempting to be addressed might ironically be made worse by the negative feedback.

For example, simply telling someone that they are difficult to work with might make them even less enjoyable to be around. (Shocking people with negative feedback is not usually an effective performance improvement plan!)

Learning to Accept Feedback

Receiving and accepting negative performance feedback in a positive way is a learned skill. It is a maturation process that needs to be developed one step at a time. An individual will be more accepting of feedback if it is received in a manner that is most comfortable to him or her. Self-directed feedback puts the individual in the "driver's seat" concerning what he or she is ready and willing to hear. It is far more beneficial for an individual to receive feedback on a limited number of factors that he or she is receptive to hearing than a full range of performance factors that he or she is not.

In Figure 16, the feedback control panel is shown, which conceptually describes the basic philosophy of self-directed feedback.

Figure 16. The Feedback Control Panel

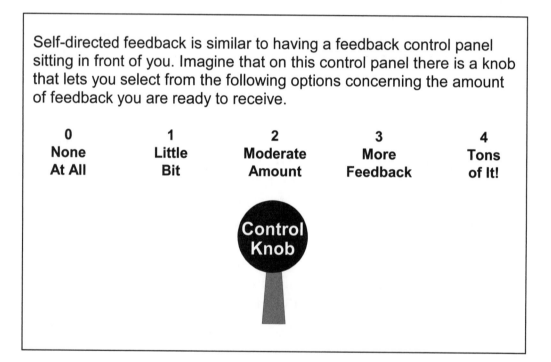

As an individual is faced with the prospect of operating this feedback control panel, he or she needs to take an introspective look at their objectives concerning feedback. If a person's main objective is to protect their self-esteem, then he or she would select the "NONE AT ALL" position on this imaginary panel. One of the most important design features of a self-directed feedback system should be this zero feedback option. Self-directed feedback recognizes the fact that there can be times and circumstances when someone just doesn't want to hear about how they are performing their job. These situations would normally be expected to occur when one is just beginning to learn a new job or might be experiencing particular difficulties.

This is not to say that people in these situations might not need or even seek guidance and direction from others; they simply don't want or need feedback on their performance during this period. However, an objective of self-directed feedback should be to have the person move his or her "feedback knob" to a level that is most beneficial to their growth and development at a later, more appropriate time.

There are other possible scenarios when a zero feedback selection might be appropriate without even a plan to move the knob, although these circumstances should be rare. One might be when a person is highly experienced and trained in a job and has no intention of changing how he or she performs their job. If providing performance feedback is nothing more than an exercise that will have no effect on performance, then obviously nothing is gained. Again, why should feedback be provided if it is not useful to anyone? It is like watching someone pound square pegs into round holes; forcing them to fit doesn't do anything except complete the task and ultimately does more harm than good.

The focus on performance feedback should be on when and where it can have the greatest impact. Let's begin to examine how self-directed feedback can help people use this information about themselves to the maximum benefit. One of the fundamental goals of self-directed feedback is to change people's paradigms about feedback. To illustrate this point, complete the following exercise about performance feedback.

Your Performance Feedback Paradigm

Instructions: Circle the answer that best applies to how you feel about feedback.

1. When I think about receiving performance feedback, I look at it as an opportunity to grow personally.

1	2	3	4	5
Never		**Sometimes**		**Always**

2. I focus more on the positives I hear as part of performance feedback than on the negatives.

1	2	3	4	5
Never		**Sometimes**		**Always**

3. If given the option, I would rather receive performance feedback about myself than not hear it.

1	2	3	4	5
Never		**Sometimes**		**Always**

4. If given the option, I would rather give performance feedback to others than not.

1	2	3	4	5
Never		**Sometimes**		**Always**

5. I feel that the performance feedback I receive is an accurate reflection of the job I do.

1	2	3	4	5
Never		**Sometimes**		**Always**

Your Performance Feedback Paradigm (continued)

Scoring:

Add up the numbers that you circled. A score of 20 to 25 would indicate that your paradigm about performance feedback is a positive one. Scores of 15 to 20 indicate your feedback paradigm is probably based on less-than-positive experiences in the past. A score of 15 or less suggests that you are not really a great fan of giving or receiving feedback.

* * * * *

Self-directed feedback can benefit most of those who scored less than 25 points on this exercise (most likely everyone who completes the exercise). An objective of self-directed feedback is to change people's paradigms of performance feedback. Changing people's paradigms about performance feedback can be a major step to making this potentially valuable communication accepted and useful to those who receive it.

In any organization, there are people on all levels carrying around their performance feedback "wounds" as a result of the KA-BOOMS they have received over the years. Self-directed feedback can help reduce the casualties of performance feedback.

In the self-directed matrix shown on the next page, you can see that two dimensions of performance feedback are being measured: the person's receptivity to the feedback and the usefulness of this feedback. Feedback that an individual might have low receptivity about receiving can still be extremely valuable. One of the objectives of self-directed feedback is to help people become more receptive to highly useful feedback on their own terms. Self-directed feedback does not support forcing this information on someone like bitter medicine before they are ready.

Self-Directed Feedback Matrix

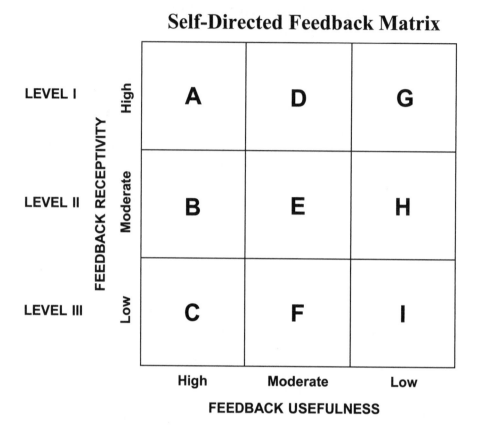

Quadrant A feedback is that which the individual is more receptive to receiving and is the most useful. Typically this is in the form of positive feedback about the individual. This type of feedback is Level I on this matrix. This feedback would serve to reinforce the positive aspects of a person's job performance. In most cases, a person's receptivity would decrease in Levels II and III in the matrix as the feedback becomes more negative or critical of the person's performance. Feedback both positive and negative can be useful to varying degrees. On the far extreme, look at Quadrant I. This type of feedback is neither readily received, nor even useful to the individual. Looking at this feedback from this perspective, one must question the value of presenting it. An example of Quadrant I feedback would be critical feedback about an individual that has little or nothing to do with the person's job performance.

What about Quadrant G feedback? Assuming that it would include positive feedback that is not particularly related to the person's job performance, is there still value in providing it? The answer to this question can be accurately addressed only with an understanding of where this feedback fits into this matrix.

Self-directed feedback needs to begin with this understanding of where feedback fits into this matrix. A self-directed feedback plan should include the individual setting goals for receiving all levels of performance feedback, particularly on the high usefulness end of the spectrum. It is also important to recognize that everyone's feedback matrix is different and unique to themselves, particularly concerning receptivity. Again, people have different tolerances and needs concerning feedback. One person might be more receptive to receiving sensitive or critical feedback than another. In developing a self-directed feedback plan, it is important to identify what quadrants you want to focus on in the process. There is nothing wrong in starting this process with goals of focusing on Quadrants A, D, and even G with hopes of moving toward Quadrants B, C, and possibly even H and F.

Designing Your Self-Directed Feedback Plan

The first question that needs to be asked when designing a self-directed feedback plan is "WHO will provide feedback to this person?" In traditional supervisor-subordinate performance reviews, it is obviously the supervisor who is the giver of feedback. And team members provide feedback to one another in team feedback. But these two types of feedback address only one level in a person's work life.

Let's examine again the newer multiple-source feedback systems being used today. 360-Degree feedback looks at the full circle of people who interact with the individual and can provide performance feedback to him or her. In these systems, individuals must accept "the complete package" of input from all sources—peers, direct reports, boss, as well as themselves.

But what if a person could choose 270-degree feedback? Or what about 90-degree or 180-degree? Self-directed feedback allows for these types of decisions to be made by the person receiving the input. The individual can choose to receive feedback from any of these sources.

Like the receptivity factor, longer-term goals for receiving feedback from a full spectrum of sources might add continuous added value and usefulness to the self-directed feedback process.

Let's look at the self-directed feedback matrix again. In this version of the matrix, we have added who provides the feedback in each quadrant.

Self-Directed Feedback Matrix
with Feedback Sources

	High	Moderate	Low
High	Boss Peers **A** Peers Reports	Boss Peers **D** Peers Reports	Boss Peers **G** Peers Reports
Moderate	Boss Peers **B** Peers Reports	Boss Peers **E** Peers Reports	Boss Peers **H** Peers Reports
Low	Boss Peers **C** Peers Reports	Boss Peers **F** Peers Reports	Boss Peers **I** Peers Reports

RECEPTIVITY (vertical axis)

USEFULNESS (horizontal axis)

Using this expanded version of the self-directed matrix, a person might first seek to receive Quadrant A feedback from a boss and Quadrant C or F feedback from a person who reports to him or her. The person might seek Quadrant D, G, or E–type feedback from his or her peers. Later on in the process, this same individual might become more comfortable receiving Quadrant B feedback from their boss and design it into their self-directed feedback plan.

A person's feedback control panel should include another "button" that controls whether the person providing the input should be identified.

Obviously in a supervisor-subordinate system, the provider of feedback is known to the receiver. However, self-directed feedback allows for the individual to decide if those providing feedback are identified or not. Obviously, this can dramatically affect the content of the feedback. Some individuals might prefer to know who is providing their feedback, while others might not. Once again, the individual completely controls the source, nature, content, and identities of the feedback received.

Using the medicine analogy to feedback once again, the individual writes their own prescription when using self-directed feedback. Most traditional performance appraisal systems attempt to give the medicine to each recipient regardless of their feedback needs. This is what could be called the "bitter pill" feedback syndrome, similar to when you were a child and your parents told you to plug your nose to avoid the bad taste of the medicine as the spoon was shoved in your mouth. Many of us grow up, believing that if the medicine doesn't taste bad, it isn't strong enough. You can apply this concept to performance feedback: "Unless the feedback is hard to receive or accept, it isn't doing its job."

All this leads to the negatively based performance appraisal systems that many organizations operate within today. These systems are based on the premise that if you only hear positives about yourself, you will never grow personally. Self-directed feedback seeks to change this feedback paradigm. Learning more about and building on your positive characteristics certainly counts as personal growth.

Most people know what they do well and what they do poorly on their jobs. We need to understand better how others perceive these abilities and characteristics. Self-directed feedback begins this process of self-exploration and discovery.

Typically we are our own worst critics when it comes to ourselves. Our own self-analysis is usually much tougher than any feedback we receive from others. These self-perceptions can serve as an excellent reference source for designing your own self-directed feedback profile, which is covered in the following section.

Developing Your Self-Directed Feedback Profile

Another goal of self-directed feedback is to go beyond the typical labeling process that is often the result of most traditional appraisal systems. Self-directed feedback is based on the belief that an individual's entire job performance cannot be accurately summarized in just one word or rating category. What is needed is meaningful and strategically directed feedback that provides information an individual can accept and apply to practical working situations. Labeling processes can cause people to perform according to expectations, often those of their supervisor. This is again like the Pygmalion effect in which other people's perceptions shape the person's own self-perceptions. In other words, if an individual is told over and over again in performance appraisal reviews that his or her performance is rated in an average category, this will become the performance standard to meet.

Self-directed feedback has the potential to allow people to set their own standards and expectations. The individual can design the process to develop his or her performance in areas in which they would like to grow. Self-directed feedback takes the concept of self-discovery and applies it to performance feedback. The ultimate objective of any feedback system is to give the individual the opportunity to learn more about him- or herself.

Labels, perceptions, resentments, defensiveness, prejudices, bias, favoritism, as well as a long list of other potentially negative factors can all influence this learning process in other forms of performance feedback. Self-directed feedback can lessen the effects of these kinds of factors, making it more meaningful to the person receiving this input.

To begin building a self-directed feedback profile, let's first look at the dimensions of performance that might be explored. We again need to start with a person's perceptions that are shaped by their performance feedback paradigm. Referring back to the exercise on pages 100–101, a low score of 15 points or less would indicate that the individual has some strong concerns about receiving performance feedback. This would in turn indicate that it would be better for this person to design their self-directed feedback to be more in the Level I range of the self-directed feedback matrix. This person might also direct their feedback to their supervisor rather than their peers, at least initially, as statistically these ratings tend to be more positive, or at least more familiar. However, this would vary depending on each person's working relationship with their supervisor and the others who might be asked to provide feedback. The object is not to "sugarcoat" the feedback that the person receives, but rather to begin changing their feedback paradigm. If the medicine tastes terrible, you will be less likely to want to take it.

Let's start by looking at the SELF Model that serves as the guiding principles for self-directed feedback.

The SELF Model

Seek
Evaluate
Learn
Follow

Seek

Self-directed feedback begins with the individual seeking the feedback. This is different than other feedback systems in which feedback is imposed on the individual, rather than sought. By putting the individual in control of obtaining the feedback, they feel less threatened by the input they receive.

Evaluate

Feedback needs to not only be presented to the individual, but also be evaluated. Quickly dismissing feedback as being inaccurate cancels out any of its potential usefulness. The individual needs to evaluate the information based on his or her objectives in seeking this feedback.

Learn

The main objective of feedback should be to learn and grow as a result. Self-directed feedback optimizes this learning process by its very nature. Learning in the form of self-exploration is its sole purpose and goal.

Follow

The most important aspect of any learning experience is what happens afterward. What will the individual do with the information received in his or her self-directed feedback process? What will follow the feedback? Will the person receiving the feedback use this information to improve his or her performance? Will they follow any advice they might receive in the process?

Self-directed feedback takes you through these steps—seek, evaluate, learn, and follow—as you progress through the process. Again, self-directed feedback puts you in charge of your own feedback. As you go through the various steps in the model, keep in mind the self-directed feedback control panel concept introduced earlier.

This first step, seek, is perhaps the most difficult for many people to initiate. Again, people tend to lack motivation when it comes to seeking feedback about themselves. The seeking phase of self-directed feedback involves the most time and effort. Unlike other feedback systems in which a standardized form or set of questions is provided, each person must design their own feedback questions and format. To help facilitate this process as well as overcome some of this inertia, the following self-directed steps model is provided.

The Self-Directed Steps Model

STEP 1

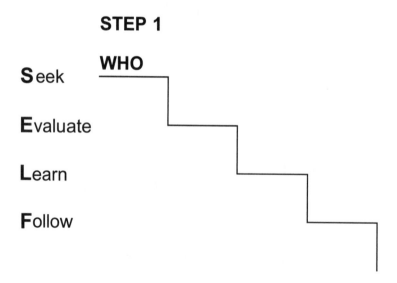

Seek

Evaluate

Learn

Follow

Step 1: Who

Deciding WHO to seek feedback from is the first step in the self-directed process. Going back to the self-directed feedback matrix with feedback sources on page 105, there are certain people who have been identified as potential sources of feedback. Each person has a defined working relationship role with the individual.

The feedback control panel pictured below depicts the people you want to ask for feedback as buttons that you push.

Self-Directed Feedback Choices

List below the WHO buttons you pushed. Also, you need to decide whether you want the people you asked for feedback to be identified, as indicated on the buttons at the bottom of the panel. Don't worry: As you proceed onto the next steps, you can go back and change the feedback sources you have selected as you begin to develop the questions you will ask these people.

The "Who" Buttons Pushed

_____

_____

_____

_____

_____

_____

_____

_____

_____

_____

_____

Step 2: What

The next part of the process is the most detailed and requires the greatest effort. Looking at the self-directed steps model, you can see the next thing to identify is WHAT performance is to be evaluated.

STEP 2

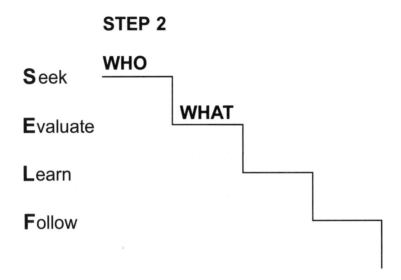

S eek   **WHO**

                 WHAT

E valuate

L earn

F ollow

There are many decisions that need to be made at this step in the process. Looking back at the self-directed feedback matrix, you now need to think about not only who you will seek feedback from, but also in what areas of your performance. Think about the WHAT in terms of the three levels of feedback: Level I, Level II, and Level III, introduced in the matrix on page 102. Your self-directed control panel would be similar to the graphic on the following page.

Sensitivity Control

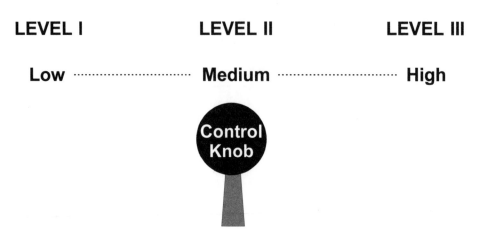

LEVEL I **LEVEL II** **LEVEL III**

Low ·········· Medium ·········· High

Control
Knob

In deciding WHAT you will seek feedback about, you need to first take an introspective look at yourself and your job performance. Most of us have a fairly accurate understanding of our strengths and weaknesses; we know what aspects of our job performance are strong and where we need to improve. The feedback we receive from others usually serves to reinforce what we already know or at least suspect about ourselves. Feedback gives us more perspectives about ourselves; self-directed feedback allows you to choose which of these perspectives you wish to get a better look at.

To help you identify WHAT you would like to receive feedback about, take a personal inventory of your strengths and weaknesses concerning your job performance.

Personal Skills Inventory

Strengths	Sensitivity Rating	Weaknesses	Sensitivity Rating

After each strength or weakness, assign a sensitivity rating of 1 to 5. Level I sensitivities are those you rated as 1, Level II ratings are those you assigned as 2, 3, or 4, and a Level III rating was given a 5.

Based on your receptivity, select those areas in which you would want to design your self-directed feedback question to address. List those areas below:

_____

_____

_____

_____

_____

_____

_____

_____

Step 3: How

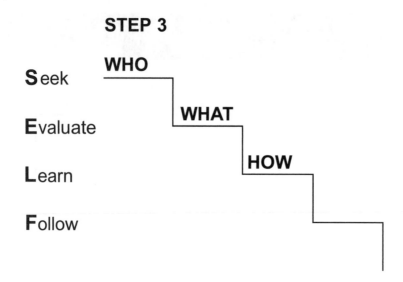

The next step is HOW. There are many HOW questions that can be asked concerning the self-directed feedback process. As is the case with other applications of the concept of self-directed feedback, many of the "How" questions are best asked by those who are involved in the process. How you will seek out the people you will ask for feedback is really up to you.

For example, most 360-degree feedback systems involve the individual mailing a questionnaire to the people from whom he or she is asking for feedback. Usually accompanying the questionnaire is a self-addressed, postage-paid return envelope to be sent to the organization that develops a profile report for the person. You could follow this approach in your self-directed feedback process, or you could ask others in person to complete the form you develop, giving you the opportunity to more clearly explain the concept of self-directed feedback. You could even develop an oral questionnaire that you read to each person. You could take notes based on this input or complete a form based on the answers you receive. You could send out your questions via e-mail or voice mail.

Another question that needs to be addressed is if the feedback is to be anonymous or identified. Obviously, interviews, e-mails, and voice mail will identify the sources of this feedback. You could find other ways in which to protect the identity of your feedback sources.

You need to evaluate how you can best process and utilize the information you receive in your self-directed process. Identifying the feedback providers will have an impact on the sensitivity of the information you receive.

Self-Directed Feedback
Control Panel

FEEDBACK SOURCE IDENTIFIER

ANONYMOUS　　　　　　　**SOURCE IDENTIFIED**

Step 4: When

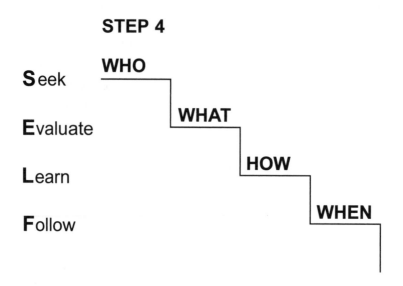

STEP 4

Seek   **WHO**

Evaluate   **WHAT**

Learn   **HOW**

Follow   **WHEN**

The final step in the model is WHEN. When do you seek feedback from others? Once a year, twice a year, whenever you feel like it? Like many other questions concerning self-directed feedback, the answer is that it is up to you. Again, looking at the self-directed feedback control panel concerning WHEN, it needs to be part of your design of the process to determine this frequency.

Self-Directed Feedback Frequency Control

Push the appropriate frequency button:

| Almost Never | Annually | Semi-Annually | Quarterly | Monthly |

Other questions that should be asked in this step include the following:

- WHEN should feedback be evaluated?

- WHEN is the best time for you to learn the most from this feedback?

- WHEN has too much time passed before evaluating the feedback, or can you react too quickly?

Perhaps the most important WHEN question is this: "WHEN do I begin my self-directed feedback process? The best way to answer this question is to go one more time to your self-directed feedback control panel. To prepare yourself for the self-directed feedback process, look at the "settings" you selected on the control panel. The answer to many of the questions you might have concerning your readiness to begin the self-directed feedback process will be found there.

One final note about WHEN. Because you are in control of the process, self-directed feedback also gives you the opportunity to talk yourself out of being ready to seek feedback. Don't let inertia keep you from seeking feedback if you are ready. Design your self-directed feedback process, and begin the process as soon as you are ready. So press the READY button on your self-directed feedback control panel and start the process.

Self-Directed Feedback Worksheet

The self-directed feedback worksheet is designed to help you use all the tools introduced in this chapter. You will find it helpful in getting you started in the self-directed feedback process. As a reference, go back to the sections in the chapter that explain each of these tools in more detail.

What were some of your self-perceptions that are important to you?

_____

_____

_____

How might they be different than the way others perceive you?

_____

_____

_____

What sensitivity setting did you dial on the self-directed feedback control panel?

_____

_____

_____

What was your frequency control?

_____

_____

_____

What was your performance feedback paradigm score? _____

Self-Directed Feedback Worksheet (continued)

Is this score consistent with your self-directed feedback control panel setting? Why or why not?

_____

_____

_____

What quadrants do you want to focus on in the self-directed feedback matrix?

____ ____ ____ ____ ____ ____ ____ ____ ____

Who are the feedback sources you wish to use in this process?

_____

_____

_____

_____

_____

_____

_____

_____

Do you want these feedback sources to be anonymous or known to you?

_____

Developing Self-Directed Feedback Questions

To help you develop your own self-directed feedback questions, the following examples are provided. These can be used as they appear, adapted to meet your needs, or modified. There are a number of ways that you can format your questions. For example, you could ask open-ended questions that would require the person providing you feedback to develop a written response. Examples of these types of questions are as follows:

1. What would you suggest I could do to improve my communications with you?

2. In which areas of my job responsibilities do you feel I am the strongest? The weakest?

3. How have I improved in my job performance since you have known me?

Or, you could ask multiple-choice questions in which the person is given a number of possible answers:

How would you describe my willingness to help others I work with?

___Not willing
___Reluctant at times
___Sometimes willing
___Usually willing to help
___Always willing to help others

Another variation of the multiple-choice answer format is to establish a rating scale for each question:

> How would you rate me concerning my ability to perform my job?
>
> | 1 | 2 | 3 | 4 | 5 |
> |---|---|---|---|---|
> | **Poor** | **Fair** | **Good** | **Superior** | **Excellent** |

At the end of your self-directed feedback questionnaire, you can also give the person the opportunity to provide any other additional information they might wish to provide to you. This can be accomplished as simply as asking for this input as shown below. However, you need to keep in mind in your self-directed feedback design that you have less control of the feedback you might receive in an open-ended question format than in the others, such as multiple-choice.

> Please provide any other comments about my job performance that you would like to share with me.
>
> _____
>
> _____
>
> _____
>
> _____
>
> _____
>
> _____

Example of a Self-Directed Feedback Questionnaire

The following is an example of a self-directed feedback questionnaire to help you in designing your own form.

Sample Cover Letter

Dear (Boss, Peer, Report, or Co-worker):

Self-directed feedback is a new way for people to receive information about their job performance. It is different than most other performance feedback systems that have set formats and distribution requirements. Self-directed feedback allows the individual receiving the feedback to make all decisions concerning the performance review process. I have designed the attached form to provide me with feedback on specific areas of my job performance that I would like to focus on at this time. Your input will be valuable in helping me grow and develop in these areas.

If you should have any questions about this questionnaire or self-directed feedback, please let me know. Thank you for your help and feedback. Please send this questionnaire back to me by _____(date)_____.

Sincerely,

John Smith

Sample Self-Directed Feedback Questionnaire

I designed the following self-directed feedback questionnaire to provide me with feedback about my job performance. Please take a few moments to complete it and return it to me in the enclosed envelope. Thank you for your help.

Sincerely,

John Smith

[Optional, depending on if you want to know feedback source(s).]

Name of person providing
feedback:_____

Please answer the following questions about me as my (check appropriate working relationship to me):

- ❑ Peer
- ❑ Colleague
- ❑ Boss
- ❑ Direct report
- ❑ Co-worker
- ❑ Business associate
- ❑ Customer
- ❑ Supplier
- ❑ Other: _____

GIVING AND RECEIVING PERFORMANCE FEEDBACK

SCALE: 0 = N/A 2 = Fair 4 = Good
1 = Poor 3 = Average 5 = Excellent

COMMUNICATIONS						
1. How would you rate my overall communications with others?	0	1	2	3	4	5
2. Do I make myself clearly understood when speaking?	0	1	2	3	4	5
3. How well do I interact with others?	0	1	2	3	4	5
4. How are my listening skills?	0	1	2	3	4	5
5. Do I seek to understand other people's point of view?	0	1	2	3	4	5
6. Do I encourage others to express their point of view?	0	1	2	3	4	5
7. Do I seek feedback from others?	0	1	2	3	4	5
8. Do I accept criticism without becoming defensive?	0	1	2	3	4	5
9. How well do I keep others informed?	0	1	2	3	4	5
10. Do I explain changes to others before they occur?	0	1	2	3	4	5
11. Do I let others know why things are being done the way they are?	0	1	2	3	4	5
12. Do I seek your opinion when making important decisions?	0	1	2	3	4	5
13. Do I give others clear expectations?	0	1	2	3	4	5
14. Do I express how I feel about important issues to others?	0	1	2	3	4	5
15. Do my actions agree with what I say?	0	1	2	3	4	5

Additional comments about my communications skills:

_____

JOB SKILLS

		0	1	2	3	4	5
16.	How would you rate my knowledge of my job?	0	1	2	3	4	5
17.	How well do I use efficient methods to perform my job?	0	1	2	3	4	5
18.	How well do I understand how my job affects other people's jobs?	0	1	2	3	4	5
19.	How well do I understand the business we are in?	0	1	2	3	4	5
20.	How would you rate the quality of my work?	0	1	2	3	4	5
21.	How well do I make others aware of what I need from them to do my job?	0	1	2	3	4	5
22.	How would you rate my enthusiasm for my job?	0	1	2	3	4	5
23.	Do I seek additional training when I need it?	0	1	2	3	4	5
24.	Do I complete assignments and tasks on time?	0	1	2	3	4	5
25.	How well do I manage priorities on my job?	0	1	2	3	4	5

Additional comments about my job skills:

_____

_____

_____

_____

_____

_____

_____

_____

INTERPERSONAL SKILLS

26.	Do I work as a member of the team?	0	1	2	3	4	5
27.	Do I help others perform their jobs?	0	1	2	3	4	5
28.	Do I convey confidence in myself and in others?	0	1	2	3	4	5
29.	Do I show respect for others?	0	1	2	3	4	5
30.	Do I show respect for the team?	0	1	2	3	4	5
31.	Do I share information important to others?	0	1	2	3	4	5
32.	Do I share responsibilities when appropriate?	0	1	2	3	4	5
33.	Do I deal with sensitive issues effectively with others?	0	1	2	3	4	5
34.	Do I help create a positive work environment for others?	0	1	2	3	4	5
35.	Do I maintain a positive working relationship with others?	0	1	2	3	4	5
36.	Do I listen for the meaning of what others say?	0	1	2	3	4	5
37.	How well do I support other people's actions?	0	1	2	3	4	5
38.	Do I put the needs of others before those of myself?	0	1	2	3	4	5
39.	How well do I maintain my working relationships with others?	0	1	2	3	4	5
40.	Do I make others feel comfortable around me?	0	1	2	3	4	5

Additional comments about my interpersonal skills:

_____

_____

TEAMWORK SKILLS

41. How would you say I work toward the goals of the team more than my own personal goals?

☐ Not at all ☐ To a limited extent ☐ When these goals are compatible ☐ Usually puts team goals before own ☐ Consistently works toward team's goals

42. Do you believe I understand the overall mission of our team?

☐ Not at all ☐ Some understanding ☐ Clear understanding of team's mission

43. How do I respond to conflicts that might occur within the team?

☐ Avoid the conflict ☐ Fight back ☐ Try to end the conflict ☐ Seek to resolve conflict, but take no other action ☐ Seek to work through the conflict positively

44. How well do I share information with other members of the team?

☐ No sharing ☐ Shares limited amounts of information ☐ Shares what is necessary ☐ Regularly shares information with others ☐ Openly shares information with everyone on the team

45. How do I accept the responsibilities of my job?

☐ Accepts no responsibilities of job ☐ Accepts only certain responsibilities of job ☐ Accepts most of the responsibilities of job ☐ Accepts all the responsibilities of job

Additional comments about my teamwork skills:

_____

_____

[**Note:** *The following questions should be sent to your direct reports.*]

SUPERVISORY SKILLS

How would you rate me concerning:

46.	My ability to give clear and understandable instructions.	0	1	2	3	4	5
47.	My supportiveness to someone making a mistake.	0	1	2	3	4	5
48.	My ability to be fair and impartial.	0	1	2	3	4	5
49.	My understanding of people's personal needs at work.	0	1	2	3	4	5
50.	My leadership abilities.	0	1	2	3	4	5
51.	My ability to create a positive atmosphere at work.	0	1	2	3	4	5
52.	My ability to deal with crisis.	0	1	2	3	4	5
53.	My ability to accurately and fairly evaluate others.	0	1	2	3	4	5
54.	My response to people's concerns.	0	1	2	3	4	5
55.	How well I communicate information.	0	1	2	3	4	5
56.	How much I trust those who work for me.	0	1	2	3	4	5
57.	How well I empower others.	0	1	2	3	4	5
58.	How accessible I am to those who report to me.	0	1	2	3	4	5
59.	How well I help people reach their potential.	0	1	2	3	4	5
60.	How I build teamwork among those in the workgroup.	0	1	2	3	4	5

Additional comments about my supervisory skills:

_____

[**Note:** *The following questions should be sent to your supervisor.*]

DIRECT REPORT SKILLS

How would you rate me concerning:

61.	How well I follow instructions.	0	1	2	3	4	5
62.	How I work toward the same goals you want me to.	0	1	2	3	4	5
63.	Sharing information with you.	0	1	2	3	4	5
64.	How I work as a member of the team.	0	1	2	3	4	5
65.	My interest in developing my job skills.	0	1	2	3	4	5
66.	My ability to adapt to change.	0	1	2	3	4	5
67.	My ability to deal with conflict.	0	1	2	3	4	5
68.	Keeping a positive attitude about work.	0	1	2	3	4	5
69.	Balancing my personal and work priorities.	0	1	2	3	4	5
70.	My commitment to performing my job in a quality manner.	0	1	2	3	4	5

Additional comments about my skills as a direct report:

_____

_____

_____

_____

_____

_____

_____

_____

_____

SUMMARY

Please provide any additional comments you would like concerning my overall job performance to include as part of my self-directed feedback process.

_____

_____

_____

_____

_____

_____

_____

_____

_____

_____

_____

_____

_____

_____

Please return this completed self-directed feedback questionnaire to me in the enclosed pre-addressed envelope within one week.

Thank you for taking the time to complete this questionnaire. If you have any questions regarding the self-directed feedback process, please feel free to contact me.

Case Study

After learning about the concepts of self-directed feedback, Jack Wilson decided to begin the process for himself. He began by completing the self-directed feedback paradigm questionnaire. He had not really given much thought before to his own perceptions concerning receiving feedback about his performance. He thought about what setting he would select regarding sensitivity on his self-directed feedback control panel. He decided that he actually had different sensitivities for receiving feedback from different people depending on their position and working relationships to him. Jack scored fairly high on the performance feedback paradigm questionnaire with a score of 19 and found this to be consistent with his other setting on his feedback control panel. He spent a considerable amount of time reviewing the self-directed feedback matrix to develop his overall feedback strategy.

He decided that he wanted to seek Quadrant A level information from his supervisor, Quadrant B from his peers, and Quadrant C from his direct reports. He also felt that some Quadrant D feedback might be useful from other co-workers. He decided he wanted all the sources of feedback to him to be identified.

The Quadrant A feedback he wanted to seek from his supervisor centered on his overall job accountabilities. He designed a series of questions to gain a better understanding of how his supervisor felt he was meeting these accountabilities. He also asked his supervisor the following question: "What would you consider to be the most important accountabilities of my job?"

He provided his peers with a number of multiple-choice questions all focused on his teamwork skills and abilities. He was concerned that due to several large projects that he had recently been assigned, that he was losing touch with these other people at work. He sought feedback from them on how he could stay in closer contact with them when working on these types of special assignments in the future.

He also realized during the past several months that the people who reported to him seemed to be upset or anxious about something lately. Even his working relationships with them that normally had been very good seemed to be strained and uncomfortable. He was concerned that this change was somehow associated with something he might be doing. Jack developed a number of self-directed feedback questions that addressed their perceptions of his leadership skills, abilities, and practices. He realized that some of their responses that he might receive could be difficult for him to hear or accept. However, he also realized that if he was to ever truly understand what might be creating this problem that he would need to put his sensitivities aside. He dove deeply into Quadrant C in the matrix to seek the feedback he felt he needed to become a better supervisor.

There was one last group from which Jack wanted to seek feedback that he felt would help him better perform his job. There were other people who worked in different parts of the organization who Jack felt did not have a very good understanding of how his department operated. He decided to ask them through the self-directed feedback process how effectively he was communicating with them concerning his department's operations and how he could improve in this area. He also wanted to seek feedback on how he could build a better relationship with others outside his department.

Finally, Jack looked at the SELF model to review what steps he needed to complete once he received this feedback. He realized that just to *seek* this feedback was not enough to achieve the results he hoped to achieve. He thought about how he needed to *evaluate* the information to really understand what he could *learn* as a result to help him improve his performance in the future. He also realized how important it would be not only to try to *follow* the advice he would receive from others, but also to follow up with possibly another self-directed questionnaire in the future to measure his progress toward achieving his performance goals.

Chapter 8

Performance Feedback Planner

As you have seen, performance feedback systems such as 360-degree and self-directed feedback allow the individual to initiate the process. You could say that this is an "inside-out" approach. Instead of the organization (outside) completely controlling the performance feedback that its employees receive, the individual (inside) becomes responsible for receiving this important information about themselves. This is truly a paradigm shift for many organizations and employees. Inside-out feedback, however, doesn't apply just to 360-degree and self-directed feedback. It also applies to any system that is initiated by the individual rather than the organization. When people accept ownership of and responsibility for their actions, it has a greater meaning and significance to them.

The following inside-out performance feedback planner is designed to help you create a feedback system of your own. As mentioned in the beginning of this book, there are no right or wrong methods of giving and receiving performance feedback. What is most important is what meets the goals and expectations of an organization and those participating in the process.

Thus, in planning your own performance feedback process, don't feel that you must employ one single source of feedback that you think would be perceived by others as the best. What is most important is what you are comfortable with and what has the greatest potential to help you improve your performance. Everything about the performance feedback planner is designed by you (inside-out). Your performance feedback planner will allow you to maximize the potential of the feedback resources that exist in your organization. Some of these resources might already exist and be part of the feedback systems that are presently in place. Your performance feedback planner can and still should incorporate these sources in order to gain the greatest potential benefit from them. Other resources might need to be developed such as a self-directed feedback, 360-degree feedback, or peer feedback processes if included in your performance feedback planner.

Your Performance Feedback Mission

The purpose of creating a personal performance feedback mission is to develop a personal statement that identifies what you plan to achieve by your performance feedback planner. Mission statements should communicate why something exists and what its purpose is in life. For businesses, mission statements usually say that their purpose is to serve their customers, providing the highest quality products or services at the lowest cost.

What is the purpose of performance feedback for you? What is it that you hope to achieve in developing your performance feedback planner? Why should it exist? How can it help you improve your performance in the future? What benefit could it be to you or to the organization? How can it improve the feedback you presently receive.

These are just some of the many questions you can ask yourself as you begin to think about your performance feedback planner mission. Obviously, performance feedback is not something that should be taken lightly or without a great deal of thought. The performance feedback you receive can be some of the most important communications you ever receive on your job. Performance feedback touches every aspect of yourself and your life. It truly does shape your future. Something as important as this deserves some planning and thought as to how it can be best achieved.

Develop your own performance feedback mission statement on the next page to give you direction as you begin your inside-out planner. Refer back to this mission frequently as you work on your planner. Constantly ask yourself this question: "Does the plan support my performance feedback mission or not?" If it does, then you are on the right track. If not, then you need to re-think the direction you might be going.

Your Performance Feedback Planner
Mission Statement

_____

_____

_____

_____

_____

_____

_____

_____

_____

_____

_____

_____

_____

_____

_____

_____

_____

_____

_____

_____

_____

_____

_____

Sources of Feedback

The next step in your performance feedback planner is to identify the various sources of feedback you might receive. This list should include both self-initiated (inside-out) forms of feedback as well as those initiated by the organization (outside-in). Note these sources in Section A: Feedback Sources.

SECTION A: FEEDBACK SOURCES

_____

_____

_____

_____

_____

_____

_____

_____

_____

_____

_____

_____

_____

_____

_____

_____

_____

_____

In sections B and C, record the aspect of your performance that you were rated highest and lowest, respectively, by these feedback sources.

SECTION B: STRONGEST PERFORMANCE AREAS

List the areas/aspects of your performance for which you received the most positive feedback.

_____

_____

_____

_____

_____

_____

_____

SECTION C: WEAKEST PERFORMANCE AREAS

List the areas/aspects of your performance for which you received the least positive feedback.

_____

_____

_____

_____

_____

_____

_____

SECTION D:

Add any additional strong or weak areas/aspects of your performance to the appropriate lists above that you would identify about yourself.

_____

_____

_____

_____

_____

_____

_____

_____

SECTION E:

Describe below any similarities, trends, or consistencies that you have identified from all these feedback sources about your performance.

_____

_____

_____

_____

_____

_____

_____

_____

SECTION F:

How can the feedback you receive be improved to help you perform your job better in the future?

_____

_____

_____

_____

_____

_____

_____

_____

SECTION G:

What do you plan to do to improve the feedback you receive in the future?

_____

_____

_____

_____

_____

_____

_____

_____

SECTION H:

How does all this feedback support your performance feedback mission statement? In other words, how will you use this feedback to support the goals you have established for receiving feedback and to help you perform your job better in the future?

_____

_____

_____

_____

_____

_____

_____

_____

_____

_____

_____

_____

_____

_____

_____

_____

_____

_____

Chapter 9

Organizational and Personal Goals

There is a great deal of focus today on the value of having the goals of the organization and its employees in alignment. This concept of organizational alignment stresses the need for everyone to be focused on the same set of goals and objectives. Everything that anyone does should support these objectives. Said another way, everyone should be "dancing to the same music."

How can performance feedback support the concept of organizational alignment? Obviously, it should play a major role in helping everyone focus on the same objectives. Often organizations compete within themselves for the attention and energies of their employees. Many times, an organization will have so many different objectives all trying to be achieved at the same time that they begin to collide with one another. It seems one goal can only be achieved at the expense of the other. This can create the trap that many performance feedback systems fall prey to today. Other responsibilities compete for the limited time there is to provide performance feedback and eventually "win" the battle for the organization's attention and focus. Besides all the many other problems that a lack of performance feedback in an organization will create, one of the most serious is the lack of measures of personal performance in relation to organizational goals. Without this feedback, people will not know if they are on target or moving away from meeting these objectives.

Even more fundamental in this discussion of organizational alignment is the need for these goals to be developed and communicated. Once established, these goals must become part of everyone's job accountabilities.

Progress made toward achieving these goals must be measured and reinforced. Competencies that people need to develop in order to meet these objectives need to also be identified and communicated. The organization must support the development of these competencies and ensure that they are measured and reinforced throughout the performance feedback process. In Figure 17, this alignment of organizational and individual goals is shown.

Figure 17. Organizational Goals Alignment

Organizational Goals

Divisional Goals

Department Goals

Individual Goals

The feedback people receive is one of the most critical factors for an organization to achieve goal alignment. This concept goes back to the SAID/HEARD—MEANT/FELT matrix. In an organization, the stated goals are what is SAID and publicized. However, what is MEANT might become perceived as something very different. You get what you reinforce.

If an organization says they want certain goals for everyone to work toward, but all the feedback systems are focused on other things, it is unlikely that these objectives will be met. Worse yet, often different levels of the organization might have conflicting or contradictory goals.

For example, an organization has a stated goal that teamwork is an important objective that everyone should be working toward. However, all the feedback, all the reinforcements, all the rewards, and all the recognition systems are focused on reaching individual accomplishments. In these circumstances, everyone quickly learns that what the organization says they want is really different than what they really want.

Figure 18 shows the way goals are perceived by people in organizations when these goals are not in alignment.

Figure 18. Organizational Goals Not in Alignment

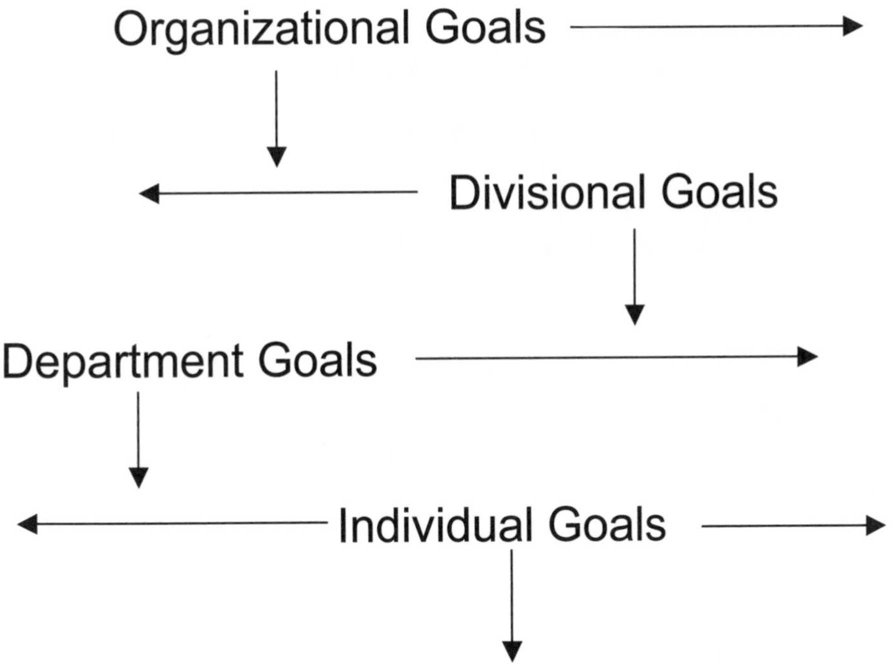

Organizational Goals ⟶

⟵ Divisional Goals

Department Goals ⟶

⟵ Individual Goals ⟶

As can be seen in Figure 18, there is almost no alignment of goals in this organization. There is a huge disconnect between what the organization says is important concerning overall performance and what finally filters down to the individual. Note in this example where individual goals are most influenced by their department: It makes sense that those you work closest with on a regular basis will have the most influence on your goals. This is because these goals are reinforced by the more frequent feedback that people receive as they perform their jobs.

Feedback is the most powerful tool that organizations have to keep everyone's goals in alignment. These goals need to begin at the top of the organization and be reinforced at every level. What the top of the organization says are important goals needs to be the same as what is heard at the lower levels. What is SAID needs to be what is MEANT concerning not only the organization's goals, but also the feedback everyone receives.

Performance Feedback as a Process

Each of the performance feedback approaches discussed in this book has the same goal in mind—to help develop the individual's overall job performance. The purpose of feedback is to provide information to people to help them better understand how to meet the requirements and expectations of others. However, receiving direct feedback from others concerning your performance is not the only way to learn and grow on your job. Actually, we learn a great deal about ourselves with every experience we encounter on our jobs. The following are just some of the many other ways that these learning experiences might be enhanced to supplement and support the performance feedback process.

Career Development Planning

Too often, career development is just something that seems to happen without a plan. It is like the analogy of setting off on a life-long journey without a map or even a destination in mind, or perhaps even worse, setting off for someplace that cannot be reached because it does not exist. Sometimes people set unrealistic goals or expectations about their careers that end up only in disappointment. This is not to say that one should not set challenging career goals or should be talked out of pursuing their dreams. Rather, one should be realistic about their career ambitions regardless of what they may be. Sometimes we expect things in a job or career that can never exist.

It is beneficial for a person to identify what their career goals are and review these goals at least annually with their supervisor or someone else who can provide knowledgeable input. In these meetings, it is important to identify developmental needs that should be addressed, as well as any obstacles to these goals that might exist. An action plan should be developed and implemented with regular update meetings scheduled to monitor progress.

Mentoring

Mentoring has received a great deal of attention in recent years as a valuable management development tool. The purpose of mentoring is to provide a key contact for an individual to meet or talk with on a regular basis in order to receive guidance and direction. Mentoring allows more experienced individuals to share their knowledge with those at earlier stages in their careers. The mentor serves the role of a big brother/sister of sorts, sharing their experience and expertise with the person they are helping. The mentor provides a "safe ear" for the individual to bounce things off from time to time. Mentors are typically outside the reporting relationship of the person they are serving; that is, the mentor is not the person who typically provides performance feedback to the person and is not part of the formal evaluation process. Mentors can provide extremely valuable feedback in this non-evaluative manner.

Training

Many training programs today include simulations, role-plays, and even feedback tools to help participants learn not only the materials presented, but more about themselves. Training programs can also provide individuals the opportunity to experience different environments and interact with different people. All these experiences provide people with new and different input. There are also training programs focusing on helping people improve their job performance skills that could be incorporated into an individual's overall developmental plan to support the performance feedback they received.

Special Assignments

Providing someone the opportunity to be on a special assignment will challenge the individual with many new experiences and require acquisition of new skills. All this provides the person with new information about how he or she responds to new situations and challenges.

Research/Reading

Sometimes the best lessons we learn in life are the ones we teach ourselves. We can learn a great deal about ourselves by our own research and reading, particularly in areas that promote self-development. Learning more about how other people succeeded can provide us with valuable insights into how we can improve our own performance.

Benchmarking

Benchmarking is a popular technique used by many organizations to improve their performance. Benchmarking involves learning more about what others do very well and then trying to emulate their performance. It is by studying the "best practices" of others that we learn to reach our greatest potential. Benchmarking is really a new term for a very old concept. After all, isn't our entire educational system based on building on the experiences and learning of those who have lived before us? Benchmarking can help an individual improve their performance by identifying other people whose skills and abilities they admire; studying what allows these people to perform in areas in which they excel; and talking to them and asking them for guidance and advice on how to develop skills in these targeted areas.

Outside Interests

Many of our personal interests outside of work teach us a great deal about ourselves. Our outside interests also provide other benefits to each of us as individuals that support our work and professional development. Outside interests provide relaxation and appropriate outlets for us to express many needs that our work might not provide. All of this can help us feel better about ourselves and the many roles we play in life, including our jobs.

Chapter 10

Performance Feedback: A Look Ahead

Performance feedback needs to look forward, not backward. Even though it seems that performance feedback is focused on reporting a person's past, it is the future that is most important. Obviously, there is nothing a person can do about the past, but the future is yet to be determined. The purpose of feedback is to help the individual improve his or her performance in the future. Performance feedback should not be a punishment for someone's past performance, but rather a tool to help them learn and grow from these experiences.

Regardless of what feedback delivery system is in place in an organization, the more involved the individual is in the feedback process, the more he or she will learn and benefit. As a result, the individual needs to be given the opportunity to be accountable for their own development. Without this accountability, even the best-designed performance feedback system will not meet anyone's expectations.

The entire organization must be supportive of the individual's efforts to grow and benefit from performance feedback. The resources needed to meet the goals set forth in performance feedback systems should be made available. Milestones striving toward attainment of these goals need to be recognized and reinforced. Most importantly, the individual must be allowed to feel good about what he or she has accomplished in accepting and utilizing performance feedback to its greatest potential.

The performance feedback paradigm in many organizations is focused on single-source systems. Usually, this is the traditional supervisor-subordinate format for delivering performance feedback. Organizations will find that using a variety of approaches to performance feedback gives people the greatest opportunity for receiving information that is most meaningful to them.

Again, there are no absolutes to performance feedback—no right or wrong ways to communicate to people how they are performing their jobs. Most important is what best fits the organization's unique culture, expectations, and values. People have many different perceptions of both themselves and the feedback they receive. The organization must provide feedback opportunities in ways that best meet the needs of everyone affected by the process. Sometimes creativity is needed to find new ways to provide and receive performance feedback. Doing this will only help the feedback process, the employees, and the organization as a whole.

The key to unlocking people's potential can often be found by providing them the type of feedback they need to grow and develop. Feedback is not something that is just nice to do, it is something that you have to do. You can't expect people to meet the expectations of others without providing them feedback about how they are progressing toward these goals. Organizations must be clear about what they want to reinforce in their feedback systems. Remember the old saying, "What gets done is what gets paid attention to."

Feedback is what shapes behaviors. We are all constantly responding to the feedback, both formal and informal, we receive in our lives. Each of us has a desire to be successful in our life and to meet or exceed the expectations of others. However, we must understand what these expectations are. Feedback is the measure of how we are doing in achieving our goals in life, both personally and professionally.

The Gift of Feedback

Don't shoot the messenger, and don't wound him either! When it comes to performance feedback, the messenger is not the enemy. The messenger in these circumstances comes to us bearing "gifts." Even though our traditional feedback and appraisal systems might make us want to return this gift for another selection, we don't really have a choice. However, this gift is ours to keep—like it or not. We need to keep in mind that gifts come in many sizes and are wrapped in different ways. We cannot accurately judge the value of a gift from outward appearances. Sometimes it takes a long time, even years, to truly appreciate the value of a gift.

Think of feedback in this same way. You might need to spend a lot of time unwrapping this gift of feedback to fully understand and appreciate its value. Don't shoot the messenger just because you don't like the feedback he or she has to bring you. You need to readily accept the messenger's feedback and reinforce him or her for this gift. Realize that this might have been a difficult experience for the messenger as well.

We are usually our own worst critics and much harder on ourselves than anyone else. The vast majority of feedback people receive is usually positive. Often we distort in our own perceptions the negative feedback we receive. Keep things in their proper perspectives and let yourself feel good about the many things you do very well and learn from those things you might *not* do so well. Don't shoot the messenger or the person receiving the message!

KA-BOOMers

KA-BOOMers are those things that people hear from others at work that make them feel like an ancient Persian messenger bearing bad news. The list of KA-BOOMers on the following page includes just a few of the countless ways that people might be made to feel at work. One of the best ways to improve the feedback that people receive in your organization is to eliminate as many of these KA-BOOMers as possible. As you read the KA-BOOMers listed, be thinking of ones you hear in your own organization.

- Quit complaining, you should just be happy you have a job.

- You should be given a lot more training than we are going to be able to provide you to do this job.

- You have a bad attitude about your job.

- You need to change your priorities.

- You don't understand the big picture.

- You don't understand how we do things around here.

- They selected someone else for the job with better "connections" than you.

- You've got to learn to play politics around here to get ahead.

- One more mistake and you're history.

- Just keep your eyes open and your mouth shut.

- If I want your opinion, I'll ask for it.

- I would like to hear what's on your mind, but I don't have time right now.

- I'm climbing to the top, and I don't care who I have to step on to get there.

- We're increasing your responsibilities, but keeping your pay the same.

- I can't recommend you for that job. You are too valuable in the one you're in.

- You need to work yourself out of a job.

- There is no such thing as job security around here.

- This information is on a need-to-know basis and you don't need to know.

- If I gave you a raise, it wouldn't be fair to everyone else.

- That's what we pay you to do.

- How would you feel about moving to....

- You'll never change my mind about that.

- We spent all that money on training you, and I still don't see any improvement in your performance.

- Are you sure this is what you want to do for a living?

- If you were doing your job right, you would not have to ask that question.

- There is no such thing as a free lunch around here.

- I don't have time to go over everything on your performance appraisal form. How about just signing it so that I can turn it in, and I'll get back to it later on.

What are some of the KA-BOOMers you hear in your workplace?

_____

_____

_____

_____

_____

_____

_____

_____

_____

_____

_____

_____

_____

_____

_____

_____

_____

_____

_____

_____

_____